# Connecting with Your Teen: The 7 Principles to Resolve Teenage Behavioral Challenges

By John P. Oda PhD, NLP

www.motivateteens.net

Dare to make
your life outstanding !!

*[signature]* John T. Oda PhD

5-24-06

DISCLAIMER

# Acknowledgements

As I reflected upon this project, I realized it was a major achievement that I needed to accomplish in my life. I feel like the Chicago Bulls of the 90's, and at times I feel like Michael Jordan when he won his first NBA championship. I have had many people shape my life in a positive way and some of their words, actions, and behaviors will stick with me forever.

First of all, I would like to thank God for giving me my talents to help people. I would also like to thank my parents Odessa and Wardine Oda for giving me support, love and guidance. Because of them, Dr. John is in the house! I would also love to thank my brothers and sister for their support. Joseph Odessa Oda Jr., Cynthia Oda, Omar Oda, Janice Oda Gray, Romaine Oda, Joyce Oda Story, Benjamin Oda, Elizabeth Oda, and Makeba Oda Moore

Special thanks goes to Sarah Godman of Portland Oregon for organizing this book, and special thanks goes to my editors, Noelle Raelson the author of *Easy Jesus* from Valparaiso, Indiana, and Rickey Pittman, author of *Red River Fever* and other books.

Much love goes to Joseph McClendon III, for giving me support, pushing me to my next level, and for being a brother, mentor, friend and someone I can count on through good times and challenging times.

A special thanks go to my Aunt Elma " Lottie" Randolph in Michigan City, Indiana, who always told me, "Stand for what you believe in" and go for your dreams.

From the mental health field, I would like to thank a man who made me believe in myself. This person took the time to work with my raw talents and in doing so he changed my entire destiny. Without this man, I would not be where I am today. I want to thank him from the bottom of my heart. I had the privilege of working with Carl Scott at Kingwood Hospital in Michigan City, Indiana and also at River Edge Hospital in Forest Park, Illinois.

Another person in the mental health field I would like to thank is Steve Goldstein. Steve has consistently given me the support I need to work in the Portland, Oregon area.

I would also like to thank Ray Shellmire, LCSW, of Portland, Oregon for helping me establish myself and giving me guidance in working with difficult clients in the mental health field.

An additional thank you to Victor Smith, of Portland Oregon, for always supporting me by giving me positive feedback, and telling me that I am going to become a great preacher someday.

I would also like to thank my success coach, Michael Leahy. Michael has supported me with publishing my book and encouraging me to go for my dreams.

I would like to thank Torrance Burrowes for helping me in the most difficult, confusing time in my life. He gave me spiritual guidance and supported my goals and dreams.

I would also like to thank Chuck Washington from Portland, Oregon, the publisher of the *Portland Observer*. He gave me my first break in writing my columns. I would like to also thank Richard Busch for giving me support and encouragement for writing in his paper, *The East County News*. By doing so, we have all helped teens change the quality of their lives.

I would like to give the most special thanks to my wife Keiko Oda, for loving me, supporting me and being my best friend. She has believed in me and encouraged me to go for my goals. I would also like to thank my additional family in Japan, Shigeru, Hiroko, and Rumiko Sawada for loving me and giving me support.

Finally, I wish to say that despite all of these outstanding influential people and their input into my work, the final responsibility for the ideas in this book rests solidly with me.

Dr. John Oda---Portland, Oregon, June 2005

This book is dedicated to my grandmother, Eva Green (1905-1977), for her love, honesty, compassion, understanding. Her love for education and wanting her grand children to be the best they can be. It was a privilege to have her as a role model at a young age. It's a true blessing to have my grandmother as an example.

To my wife, Keiko, the woman of my dreams, my best friend, my better half. The person who kept me grounded and humble, and supported my dreams. I love you forever.

To my friends, Allan Magbanua, Luis Bengero, and Dave Lopez of twenty years or more who have given me encouragement, support and love.

I give thanks to God for giving the ability to help people, to make a difference in people lives. To share my passion, my love to serve others in the highest way.

# Table of Contents

# Foreword by Joseph McClendon III

It has been said many times and in many ways that the future holds untold promise and abundance for all of us. Our attitudes, our work ethics, our self-esteems and our belief systems all contribute to what we can and will make of our lives.

In general, the earlier we receive positive influence, and more specifically, the earlier we accept and execute the lessons of that positive influence. The faster we build a life that we can be proud of and one that contributes to the betterment of our families and the ones we love.

In short, the earlier we learn life's most important lessons and the earlier we put them into practice. The easier we make our lives. At the very least, we enhance our availability to be the recipients of what is possible for the future.

There is not a parent on the planet who doesn't want the very best for his or her children. There is not one teacher or coach that doesn't want to shorten the semesters of the school of hard knocks for their students. We all want them to learn what we already know sooner and to avoid some of the mistakes that could cost them so very much in the future. As parents we want to be able to accept that communication and at the very least consider it.

Although communication skills are certainly the better part of the solution, they are not the complete solution. Learning to be a more effective communicator on the part of the parent or teacher is the key to achieving measurable dynamic results.

I've known Dr. John Oda for over a decade now, and besides being a peak performance expert, a tireless advocate for teens and their parents, and a concerned therapist and personal coach that helps others make breakthroughs, I have found him to be a friend. Tirelessly, he consistently gives of himself, often making believers out of clients who come to him having never believed in themselves or their abilities.

Dr. Oda's principles can be life-changing if you will have faith. Through his program you will begin to transform your life as you simply begin to believe more and more in yourself and your abilities to influence yourself and others.

Dr. Oda is a peak performance expert specializing in assisting others in getting the best out of themselves. Certified in Neuro Linguistic Programming and several other techniques, he pays close attention to the social and emotional influences that impact our youth. Dr. Oda's approach is unique and effective.

Through stories and examples, Dr. Oda weaves lessons that hit home for all of us. He tells the story of one teen who made poor choices and wrecked his life and how he longed to make the opposite choices. In another scenario he shows the same teen making the better choices and how much happier he is. This serves as a warning and a rallying cause for the importance of connecting with your teens. Luckily for us the readers, he next shows us his Seven Principles for Connecting with Teens and how important this is. Now, just these principles alone would be well worth the cost of this book, but Dr. Oda doesn't stop there.

Drawing upon his many years of clinical practice in in-patient and out-patient settings, as well as private practice where he has worked with thousands of teens and kids, he relates tragic, gut-wrenching studies of teens who reached critical turning points in life. He describes their cases, and drives home his points about how his principles could have made a difference and illustrates powerfully how he used the principles in working with these challenging cases. He shows you cases where lives have been changed and transformed.

You too will find yourself transformed and changed if you as a parent or other caregiver of teens and kids will apply just some of the principles in this book. I heartily recommend it and encourage you to learn how to better connect with your teens and show them the love and affirmation that they need to help them face the many challenges that exist in our current age. In the process, your life will be changed, I guarantee it!

-----------------Joseph McClendon, III, Head Trainer for the Anthony Robbins Organization, UCLA instructor, co-author of two best sellers *Unlimited Power the Black Choice* and *Power Thoughts*.

# A Teen Story

Allan Private was a high school senior unhappy with his performance in academics. He did not get along well with his parents and had attempted suicide several times. A mental health worker told his family that Allan had low self-esteem and lacked self-worth, thereby inhibiting his ability to love himself.

Allan's teachers told the family that he was failing all of his classes due to hanging out with the "wrong crowd," skipping school and not handing in his homework. Allan told his parents that his only focus in life was partying with his friends and doing drugs. He wanted an escape from his unsuccessful life, the yelling and fighting in his home, and his own apathy.

One night he went to a rave with some friends, the biggest party of his high school career. Everyone was drinking and using drugs, including Allan. After partying for a while, Allan felt like going home. He got into his car and sat overlooking the city. His shoulders slumped and his head hung low.

He thought about all of the wasted time and energy he had put into his family and school. He blamed his parents for not supporting him. He blamed his school for demanding homework and studying. He blamed his old friends from grade school for moving ahead and leaving him behind.

He started his car and made his way home. He felt like his world was spinning like a top. His vision was blurred and his body was drenched in sweat. He could not control an intense sensation moving through his body.

Stepping on the gas, Allan drove the car faster and faster, trying to get home quickly in order to stop this overwhelming feeling. He was filled with fear and anger, leading to poor impulse control. He went through several red lights, and finally as he ran through one, there was another car, a collision, and then darkness.

Eventually, he lost consciousness of the external world, leaving him feeling internally different. Pain filled his body. Allan could see everything around him as though he were in a dream. There were ambulances, tow trucks and people crying over dead loved ones. Allan could hear his friends talking amongst each other, pitying him and hoping he did not die. He could see himself lying on the ground, with the firefighters across the way sawing through the other car to remove the dead passengers.

Then, he saw two paths to take, and realized that he was about to start his journey. Allan was taking the easy road while the other path seemed entirely too difficult—full of hard work and requiring persistence. Allan decided on the easiest route. The first path led him into a dark tunnel and once through the tunnel, a bright light shone in his eyes.

Allan awoke from his dream in a hospital bed with a doctor standing over him asking questions: "What's your name? Where do you live? What is the date? Who is the President of the United State?" Allan replied, "I think its March 20$^{th}$, 2005. George Bush." The doctor appeared confused and asked the questions again, to which Allan provided the same answers.

While the doctor checked his vitals, Allan asked for his parents. The doctor explained to him that he had been in a very bad car accident and had been drinking. His son was in the car with him and did not survive. He went on to say that is was the year 2030 and he did not know where Allan's parents were.

Just then, a frantic woman came bursting into the room screaming at Allan. Hospital attendants rushed to hold her back as the middle-aged woman yelled that Allan had killed her baby and she wished that he had died instead. The woman had a hard face, as though she had been drinking for much of her life.

Allan was confused; he did not know what to say or do. He asked himself: "What has happened to my life? How did I end up with so much pain and sorrow? How did I create a life so messed up?" The doctor interrupted his thoughts, telling him to rest, but Allan just wanted to go home and find out what was going on.

Allan asked his girlfriend, Carol, who was by his hospital bed, to take him home. On their way home, Carol complained and made excuses for why her life turned out so badly. She blamed society for why she was poor and had mental challenges. She faulted society for ruining her chances to succeed.

Once they arrived home, four poor-looking children ran out of the house without shoes on their feet. Carol yelled at the children to get away, and they ran off quickly. Once inside, Allan was eager to learn of how his life got to be this way, but Carol just wanted to get drunk and high. Allan sat there asking himself how he could be in a relationship like this.

Allan asked himself why he would be in a relationship like this. Allan's friend Ken stopped by the house. He said, "Man you are one lucky guy. I am happy to see you alive." Allan explained to Ken that he doesn't remember his life, and asks him if he can explain to him what happened.

Ken explains to Allan that they went to high school together, and after his accident when he was eighteen years old his life changed. Ken explains to Allan that people died in that accident and Allan's life went downhill. Ken explains to Allan that at twenty-three years old, he was a very abusive guy toward his girlfriend. He yelled, screamed, and sometimes hit her. He was a very negative complainer and never had a real job. He always wanted people to take care of him

Ken also told Allen that he lived in an old barn, where he had parties all night. Ken explains to Allen that he appeared old looking. It seems like he had a rough life, and the drinking and partying was too much for him.

*Why did Allan make the wrong choices? What can Allan learn from his mistakes?*

1. *Have a personal mission statement.*
2. *Whatever you focus on, you will become.*
3. *Raise your standards.*

Ken, continued, saying that in his late twenties, Allan gained an unhealthy amount of weight, around 60 pounds, and always appeared depressed. Allan had also attempted suicide several times. He exhibited an explosive rage towards people. At times, he was homeless and would dig through garbage for food. Allan had even been a male prostitute, selling his body for money to buy drugs. Most of his friends were in jail, prison, or dead. Upon hearing all of this, he felt horror and shame, realizing that the people he had associated with dictated his own standards of living. He was disgusted with himself and wanted to go back in time.

Suddenly, Allan felt sick to his stomach. He told Ken that he was getting tired and wanted to get some rest. As he fell asleep, he thought, "I know how to change my life. Please give me a second chance."

Once asleep, a visible force guided Allan to a funeral where his family was present. Allan listened to the pastor read out the short obituary and it seemed like the deceased had not accomplished much in his life. Allan asked the guide who the funeral was for. The guide turned to him and said, "Allan Private," pointing to the tombstone that read, *Allan Private. 1982-2030.* Allan begged the force to take him home. The guide told Allan that he could not return home until he met another guide, and that this guide would bring closure to his past.

Allan asked himself a powerful question: "What must I do to change my life now?" A voice inside his head replied, "Your thoughts, words and actions are creative. So whatever your thoughts are, your feelings and actions will follow and produce the results of your life."

*What can Allan learn from his past?*

*1. To change your environment, meaning the people you associate with.*
*2. Monitor your thoughts, words and actions because they create your destiny.*

Allan fell asleep and met another guide in a dream. He came upon a dark tunnel, and once at the end, a white light again shone in his face. He was in a hospital bed and a doctor was asking him questions. "What is your name? Where do you live? What is the date? Who is the president of the United States?" Allan replied, "March 20th, 2005. George Bush." The doctor again asked him the same questions, and Allan provided the same answers. The doctor told Allan that he had head injuries and possibly swelling on his brain, causing a lapse in his memory. The doctor ordered more tests to determine the cause of why Allan was mentally in the past.

Allan turned and saw a grey-haired old man standing at his bedside. The old man said to Allan, "I don't know why you drive those antique cars when we have more advanced ones. I am so happy that you will be better in a couple of days, though." The old man told Allan that his wife and children were coming back from Africa because they had heard the news of his condition.

Allan asked the elder man, "Who are you?" The elderly man replied, "My name is Timothy, your driver. You don't remember me sir? The doctor was right, your brain must be swollen and you've lost your memory." Allan was very upset and angrily said to Timothy, "Let me ask the questions! Tell me what I want to know!"

In the background the radio was reporting the news: "Billionaire Allan Private was in a car accident today. Mr. Private is a real estate developer owning private plazas in Las Vegas, Chicago, New York, and all around the world. The company released a statement indicating that CEO Allan Private was not seriously injured and should be better in a few days"

Allan listened quietly, shocked about the news he had just heard. Allan told Timothy to turn on the television to see if there was more information on the news. Timothy flipped to a news channel where Allan watched a report on himself on television, and was amazed at the amount of respect he received from the media. Allan asked Timothy to get him a mirror. When he saw his reflection in the mirror, he was surprised. He appeared to be in good health, and noticed that he had aged well, obviously taking good care of himself.

Timothy interrupted Allan, saying, "Mr. Private, the press is outside the hospital. It would not be in your best interest to speak to them at this time in your condition. I'm going to speak to your doctor about insuring confidentiality."

Allan told Timothy that he wanted to go home immediately despite the doctor's orders to stay in the hospital for a couple of days. At Allan's insistence, Timothy drove him home in a Mercedes limousine. They arrived at a beautiful mansion. Realizing that this is where he lived, Allan wondered how he could have created something so wonderful, after having grown up in such a terrible environment. Timothy got out of the limousine first, and then opened the door for Allan. They proceeded to the front door of the house and stepped inside the magnificent mansion with marble floors, a large crystal chandelier and photos of a family on the walls. The people in the photographs appeared to be very happy and in love. Allan was curious to find out how he had created such a loving family that appeared to respect each other. He began asking Timothy several questions about his life.

Timothy explained that after Allan's first accident as a teen, Allan promised to serve others in the highest regard. After taking another life in the accident and seeing the pain the others went through, Allan changed his life for the better. He worked his way through college, as well as holding down a fulltime job. In college, he met and fell in love with his wife. Allan created personal principles to bond with his children and have a lasting relationship with his wife. Allan was very impressed that he was able to give back to society and create an outstanding family.

At that moment, the door opened and his wife, Carol and their children came into the house. Carol ran towards Allan, embracing him and asking him if he was okay. The family seemed so excited to see him. They told him that they took the private jet back to make sure that he would be fine. Allan felt like the luckiest man in the world as Carol looked at him with so much love in her eyes. Allan soon learned that he had two sons, Jerry, ten years old, and Allan Jr., twelve years old, as well as two daughters, Susan, fifteen years old, and Elizabeth, sixteen years old. His children seemed very loving and happy.

Allan sat at the table with his family, holding Carol very tightly. They looked through old photos of their younger years together and videos of the family's vacations. Allan began to understand the meaning of life and that this was the life that he wanted to live. Carol gave Allan a small necklace and told him to put it around his neck. The necklace was from France, and would bring him luck. Carol joked that Allan could use all the luck he could get with his driving record.

Allan did not want the night to end; he wanted to be with his family like this forever. As they watched videos through the night, Allan fell asleep in Carol's arms. While he slept, he sensed that it was time to move on, and a strange, overwhelming feeling came over his body. He knew he was leaving this moment, and wished he could take all that he had learned back with him to change his life. He awoke with a white light shining in his face, and once again was in a hospital bed, with a doctor asking him questions. The doctor told Allan that he had been in a car accident, and a passenger in the other car he hit, had died. His parents were on their way, and should be there soon.

Allan thought that all the events he had seen in his future had been a dream, until the doctor showed him an expensive necklace that they had removed from his neck. Allan looked at the necklace and recognized it as the one

Carol had given him. He realized that it all was not a dream and understood that he had a choice in his life and that he must create his own destiny.

Allan explained to the guide that he didn't want to live that kind of life. He asserted that there must be another way to live. Then the guide told Allan that on earth you can do one of two things, you can serve others, or others can serve you.

Allan asked the guide what he meant by those statements. The guide explained that you can chose to treat people with respect, have an attitude of gratitude and serve others. Or you can complain like most people do in life, and be angry and mistreat others. The tables can turn meaning you can have others serve you. Meaning you can be in a wheel chair, in a coma depending on someone else to take care of you. People can treat you, like you treat them. The guide explained to Allan that everyone has choices in life and now, since he has seen his future, what path would he take?

**Study Questions**

1.  What did you learn from the story?

2.  What path is your teenager taking?

3. Is your teenager becoming the victim? i.e., complaining and not taking responsibility for their actions?

4. What is your family focus? Whatever you focus on, you will feel. If you only focus on the negative that is going on in your household, that is what you will create in your life. Remember the story of Allan Private and his focus on the negativity in his life. How can you make a change in your life today?

5. How can you raise your standards? Instead of saying, "Do I have to?" say "I get to." Instead of saying, "Should I?" say "I must." Write down some ways to raise your standards for yourself and for your family.

6. Is your teenager making the right choices?

7.  How can you use the information from this story to empower your family? How can your teen change his/her environment in a positive way?

8.  What positive changes can you make in your family today?

9.  What is your family's mission statement? Have your entire family sit down to create a statement that defines your family in a positive way.

# The 7 Principles for Connecting to Your Teen

**Principle 1**: Teach your child something of value and a sense of purpose.

When Allen was growing up, his parents did not teach him anything of value, but instead, enforced many rules. They just told him what he should do. Teach your children value. For example, if you want them to go to college, you must explain to them why an education is important. You can tell them the more they learn, the more they will earn. Let them know that you want them to have a better life than you had. With an education, they will have more opportunities to choose from.

1.  What values can you teach your children?

2.  What reason or purpose can you give them for these values?

3.  How can this concept impact your own life?

**Principle 2**: Find one activity to do with your children.

While growing up, Allan made excuses to avoid being around his parents. Although they sometimes connected, the majority of the time, Allan could not stand to be around them. It seemed to him that they were always complaining about something. After his vision with the guides, he realized that he was missing a positive connection with his parents. He only had an unhealthy relationship with them, which included fighting, yelling and general disrespect.

Allan actually used drugs and alcohol as a coping method around his family. When he was drunk or high, he was not concerned about his actions towards his parents. He later realized that this was an unhealthy escape from dealing with reality.

As parents, I urge you to take an active interest in your teenager's life. Find one activity you can do with your children; it can be simple, yet special and unique to your relationship. Activities could include taking a trip together, attending a sporting event or a concert. When you find that one thing that connects you to your child, give them all of your attention.

1.  What can you do with your children that will connect you to them?



2.  How would this impact your relationship with your child in a positive way?



**Principle 3**: Parents should do something for their child that is not materialistic.

I have interviewed many teens in my seventeen years of counseling. Their number one complaint is that most parents buy them clothes and send them on trips, but actually spend little quality time with them!

In the story, Allan had no connection with his parents. The only interaction they had was through yelling and fighting. Parents should explore the positive connections they could have with their children. This means thinking in new ways and engaging in new behaviors to establish healthy patterns. For example, thinking of different ways to communicate with your teenager, such as through physical touch. Even a touch or a pat on the back can help you communicate with your child on a personal level. Personal contact improves bonding. Perhaps out of embarrassment, parents tend to think their children outgrow the need and desire for closeness. On the contrary, children are never too old for a hug. While they may be embarrassed at this personal contact in front of their peers, in a more private setting, it is a welcome gesture.

I held a workshop in Portland, Oregon, emphasizing the need for parents to connect with their teenagers. I found that most parents did not find creative ways of connecting with their teenagers; however at this workshop, parents shared different ways they found to make a connection. One parent in the group said that she gives her son back massages and he returns the favor. Another parent said that she does her daughter's nails. These favors help to improve the parental-child relationship greatly.

Connecting with your child does not require a great deal of money. There are numerous ways to connect with your teenager without spending any money. Find 10 creative ways to connect with your teenager that you can practice at home.

List your ideas below:

1)
2)
3)
4)
5)
6)
7)
8)
9)
10)

**Principle 4**:  Give your child something that belongs to you.

Giving your child one of your belongings will help establish a connection. For example, lockets, bracelets, necklaces and rings that have personal meaning to you are a part of you.

1.  What can you give your child that is a part of you?  Explain the significance of the item in detail.

2.  How can you enjoy this process?

3.  How does this teach your child to give?

**Principle Five**:  Engage your teenager in conversation.

Sometimes it seems difficult to relate to your teenager, but that is how you find out the most about them.  At times, it may feel like you are from an entirely different planet or era.  How many parents engage their teen in daily conversation that does not include yelling?  Here are some questions you can use to get started:

1.  *How are you feeling?*
    If your teen simply says "okay," dig a little deeper.  This means asking them what has happened in order for them to feel a certain way.  Find out exactly what they are feeling.

2. *What's going on in school?*

   It is important for parents to find out what is happening in their child's school life rather than having a teacher give them a call to report. Ask your teenagers what their favorite classes and who their favorite teachers are. Find out what classes are challenging for them. In Allan's story, his parents did not know what was going on with his schoolwork, his friends, or even his attendance at school. Take charge of your teens.

3. *Who is your best friend these days?*

   Many parents have never even met their children's friends. As a parent, you need to find out whom your child hangs out with. Remember, birds of a feather flock together. Your child will mimic his/her surroundings. Find out about your children's friends, and try to meet their parents as well.

4. *What are your hobbies?*

   If your child plays sports or and an instrument, you could use this as an opportunity to spend time with your child doing what he/she likes. By finding out what your teenager's interests are, you can find ways to connect with them and do activities together.

5. *How many friends do you have and how do they treat you?*

   Find out how many friends your teenager has, and how these friends treat him/her. Find out if peers tease your child, or if your child teases others. Note: Some teens may not have *any* true friends.

Provide your child with all of your attention when asking these questions. Do not pick up the phone, or stare at the television or computer screen while talking to them. Making eye contact with your child and taking part in a caring "give and take" style of conversation shows your child that you are listening and they have your support. Keep encouraging more conversation. Use open-ended questions that cannot simply be answered with a *yes* or a *no*.

By asking these questions, you are finding out about your child's life. Many teenagers have expressed that it seems their parents do not have time for them or get to know them enough to have a non-condescending conversation. Make sure not to lecture your children when you are trying to connect with them.

Find someone that you can role-play with and practice these tools. Make this into a game and remember to have some fun with it.

**Principle Six**:  Tell your children that you love them.

Do not say to yourself, anyone else and especially to your children, "They know I love them, so why should I tell them?"  Imagine if your teenager did not know if you loved them or not because you never said that you did.

I worked with a sixteen-year-old young man, "Mike," who was fighting with his father and getting into fights at school.  His father said that he needed help with his anger and drug use. Mike came to the hospital where I was working for several days and participated in a self-esteem group I facilitated.

At one group, Mike shared with the group that his father never told him that he loved him in his life.  His mother had died several years earlier and Mike felt like he had no one to talk to about his feelings.  His father only seemed to yell at him. The only way he found to deal with his hurt and anger was using drugs and drinking. Mike was extremely depressed. He later told his peers at the hospital that he would kill himself, which they kept to themselves.

One day, after having a shouting fight with his father on the phone, Mike committed suicide. Imagine being Mike's parent.  Imagine your child dying without you saying to them "I love you."  Mike's father felt extensive guilt, pain, and loss.

Following this incident, I always emphasize to parents at my seminars the importance of telling your child that you love him/her. During one seminar, a grown man in the audience said that his father never told him that he loved him, and in turn, he never told his children he loved them.  He believed that they could just tell from his actions. This man later emailed me and reported that he told his daughter he loved her for the first time in twenty-one years. This took his daughter by surprise and initiated a much better relationship between the two of them.

From working in this field for seventeen years, I have heard many parents say, "You know I love you" to their children, but they fail to state it plainly in both actions and words.  Children need to hear that their parents love them over and over and they need to see it as well in their parents' actions. Teenagers may also not verbalize that they love their parents; however, if parents continuously do this, their children are much more likely to return the sentiment.

Now is the time to tell your teenager how you feel about them in a positive light. Describe what would happen if you did not tell your teenager that you loved him/her. What would it cost you? How would you benefit from telling your child, "I love you"?

**Principle 7:** Have an attitude of gratitude.

My last principle is one that everyone should practice, regardless if they have children or not. Occasionally, you will have challenges with your children and they may push your stress levels. Additionally, it is difficult to not constantly worry about your children's safety with all the violence in our society; however, some people forget to be thankful for the health and safety of their families.

Every parent should have an 'Attitude of Gratitude List.' This list can include good aspects about your children that your write down every morning and/or night. One of my clients in Portland, Oregon, had such a list with the following statements: "I am happy that my child is alive. I am happy that he is going to school. I am happy that he is coming home to eat. I am happy that he is healthy. I am happy that my child is walking and talking. I am happy that my child is breathing on his own. I am happy that my child is working on himself. I am happy that my child is coming home safely today and for his helping around the house. I am happy that my child is waking up with the right mindset and all of his bodily functions are working." My client would read this list daily to reinforce her attitude of gratitude.

Now make your own list so that you can exhibit an attitude of gratitude for your children.

**To review, the "The Seven Principles to Connect with Your Teen" are:**

1. Teach your child something of value and a sense of purpose.
2. Find one activity to do with your children.
3. Parents should do something for their child that is not materialistic.
4. Give your child something that belongs to you.
5. Engage your child in conversation.
6. Tell your children that you love them.
7. Have an attitude of gratitude.

## A Letter from a Parent

Dear John:

They say that the definition of insanity is doing the same thing over and over again yet expecting different results. We not only did the same thing over and over again with our twelve-year-old misfit, we did everything over and over again. Positive reinforcement, negative reinforcement, immediate consequences, years of psychoanalysis, you name it. No sale. He returned immediately to his apparent hard-wire set point of shirking responsibility, blaming everyone else for his failures, glowering negativity, lying etc. We were out of options, exhausted from propping him up against the inevitable failure that seemed destined for him.

A chance meeting with you led to our enrolling our son in your seven-week workshop, "The Seven Techniques of Highly Self-Motivated Teens," and (later) "Bonding the Family Together." In spite of our burned out skepticism, we noticed subtle changes in his attitude immediately. By the second week, it was as if metabolism had sped up. He was actually doing his homework unprompted, and pitching in on household chores. We are actually enjoying his company. Yesterday, he gently chided me for my chronic "negativism" while driving. He was right. We are witnessing what appears to be nothing less than a transformation. John, you are a miracle worker.

Sincerely,

Tom, Portland Stepfather

# Rapport Skills

Besides the powers of unconditional love and affirmation, building rapport is among the most powerful tools a parent can utilize, as it creates bonding power. Having rapport with your teen makes him/her feel very open and comfortable, and a strong rapport elicits teens to trust their parents. Rapport is like a lovely dance, in which everyone is on the same beat.

Here is an example of good rapport in parenting:

- Two mothers, each with a sixteen-year-old daughter, with both parents having the same educational levels and living in the same part of town. One parent, Janice, and her teen always seem to be arguing and not getting along. The other mother, Karen, and her daughter are very much on the same page. They talk about their challenges, communicate very well and trust each other. What is the difference? The major difference is that Karen has found ways to build a solid rapport with her teen, by matching her communication patterns to those of her daughter. Karen creates an atmosphere of mutual liking, trust and understanding with her daughter. Karen is able to do this authentically, without pretense, out of love for her daughter and her efforts transcend mere semantics.

## Achieving Rapport

Rapport is achieved when two people are on the same page and appreciate each other's feelings. Have you ever been to a social gathering where you met someone with whom you felt a special connection? You catch yourself sensing that you seem to have the same things in common, or it seems like you have known this person all your life. That is rapport.

Many non-verbal components to communication exist. Body language is often the strongest cue and the easiest to observe. Our posture, hand movements, breathing, voice patterns, tone, tempo and tonality are all non-verbal aspects of communication. All of these qualities can be used in both establishing and maintaining rapport. Throughout our lives, we have seen the unconscious body language of people around us. As a parent, you can take this knowledge and use it to consciously build rapport with your teen, and guide your child to your belief system.

If you have ever watched *Oprah*, you have likely observed in her audience a wide variety of behaviors, including breathing rates, body posture, facial expressions, eye movement and tone of voice. You can gather a wealth of information about those people without ever meeting them.

### Bonding with Your Teenagers

Imagine how it would be to truly bond with your teenagers. How would it feel to have the same mindset, have the same respect and appreciate each other's point of view? How powerful would these techniques be to a parent?

As a parent, you have the power to learn how to tap into these resources. With practice, you can understand these techniques so you can establish rapport with almost anyone. This is a powerful tool to enhance communication. Imagine what might happen if you did not learn how to gain rapport with your teen and someone else does, such as a drug dealer, a gang member or anyone applying peer pressure?

My goal is to give you enough information to build rapport with your teen. Having rapport creates an atmosphere of:

- Trust
- Confidence
- Cooperation

With these three factors set in motion, your teen can and will respond freely.

### Benefits of Rapport

A key benefit of rapport is establishing **sameness,** a sense of moving through time together. Do you want to find a way to communicate with your teen, to gain their trust, confidence, cooperation, and participation? This does not demand identical worldviews. Rapport simply creates a sense of shared understanding. Your teen will feel so connected to you that he or she will naturally gravitate towards your values. In the old days, psychologists called this the development of the superego, that children would reflect or unconsciously adopt the values of their parents. Beyond this, a sense of sameness will help your teen know that he/she always has someone to talk to, that his/her parent is actually there for support and understands his/her adolescent challenges.

In studying how to obtain rapport, it is first necessary to listen to your teens, asking for clarification if you do not understand them. Match your listening skills with observations of your teen's behaviors. Please make it a point to observe and listen to everything they say! For example if your child use the word "outstanding" in his/her sentence, when you speak, use the same word. This will result in your child feeling more connected to you.

Notice how your child behaves in each and every situation, what he/she says about the situation verbally and with body language and attitudes. For example, observe your child around friends, at birthday parties, school, sporting events and places where teens interact.

When you are truly tuned in to your teen and clearly understand him/her, you have the greatest opportunity to establish rapport. It will also require a loving, understanding and compassionate heart. Observe that when people are in rapport, **their communication takes on a pattern of the dance.** It's rhythmical: their words and their bodies match each other smoothly and easily. When people are in rapport, they unconsciously mirror, match and pace each other.

### Mirroring

When people are mirroring each other, they adopt the same physical posture and mannerisms. Mirroring happens when you copy the behavior of others, thus you are a reflection of that other person. For example, a person crosses his right leg over his left leg, and you cross your right leg over your left leg (in the field of psychology, we call this "synchronization").

When you are in "deep rapport" with another person, mirroring often occurs at the unconscious level, without conscious thought. As a parent, you will often see this if you watch your teens with their best friends. When they mirror each other, they do it so smoothly, naturally. They adopt the same posture, body movement and mannerisms. They talk about the same topics most of the time, and they do it effortlessly, like they have known each other forever.

By the same token, it is difficult to have a conversation with someone whose body language is very different from your own. If your teen is standing with his or her arms closed and yours are open, this might pose a challenge. By using their bodies in this way, they are telling you in no uncertain terms that they do not feel a connection to you.

When mirroring your teens, you are offering them an unconscious reflection of themselves. This simple technique has a very powerful impact because the way your teen responds to the mirroring is in effect a response to his/her own behavior. (This can eventually give them insight into their own behaviors.)

Mirroring can also be used to reinforce a good or desired behavior. For example, when teens observe parents reflecting their behavior on an unconscious level, they feel a sense of connection. Your teen can feel like you know where he/ she is coming from and that he/she can talk to you about anything.

### Matching

Matching occurs when your behavior is the same as your teen. For instance, if your teen crosses one leg over another, you can do the same thing (or a similar thing) a few seconds later. The movements are enough alike for your teen to feel connected you, but different enough that they will not feel you are **mimicking** them.

Matching your teen should flow naturally and effortlessly while you are in communication with them. If your teen taps his pen on the desk, a parent could tap his foot in the same rhythmic way. The teen's unconscious perceives your movement as a reflection of the teen's unconscious actions.

For example, I had a teenager, who would frequently tap his pen to the beat of a song. I would repeatedly explain to him that we were in group therapy and asked that he please do this at another time. He would agree, but in a couple of seconds he would resume the tapping. The next day, he came to group and I had to tell him to stop again, but then I started tapping my feet to his same beat. The teen responded by stopping the tapping of his pen and we had a magnificent session.

### The Results of Rapport

The outcome of creating rapport is to connect with the unconscious, and to get in the same mindset as your teen. Matching the physiology of your teen is one of the simplest ways to do this. This means matching breathing patterns and voice tone patterns as well.

Some people do this on an unconscious level (without knowing what they are doing). Again, watch two people who are best friends; they almost act the same, possibly moving their bodies the same way. Friends may display similar, if not the same type of mannerisms, because they are in synch with one another.

Everyone has a different type of voice, but it is best to match your teen's voice as closely as possible. Watch for the tone, (whether it is low or high), tempo (speed of speech) and tonality of your child's voice. This is a very powerful way to gain rapport with your teen. Listen also to the volume, tone, pitch and rhythm of your teen's words in addition to their voice.

Another way to gain rapport with your teen is, matching your teen's physiology. This includes matching your teen's breathing pattern and their hand movements. This can be very powerful because this is an unconscious process that usually goes undetected. When we perceive that someone matches our breathing, it creates a bonding of trust and understanding. We start to relate to that person on an unconscious level.

### Overview of Rapport

When creating rapport, mirroring and matching your communication style with that of the teen you are communication with is essential. The elements of effective mirroring, matching and pacing include:

- **Physiology**—Matching body position (mirroring and pacing also play a role), breathing, voice, gestures and hand movements.
- **Movements**—Matching what your teen does in regard to the types or kinds of movement and gestures used.

- **Strategies**—Matching how your teen undertakes activities and thinks.
- **Tone, Tempo, and Tonality**—Matching voice, pitch and the rhythm of your teen's words.

When observing people who are in rapport, it has been observed and documented that the greatest similarities were in the areas of:

- breathing
- voice tone and tonality
- posture, body movement and gestures
- language content and use of key words
- visual/auditory/feeling cues
- beliefs
- values

# Using Music/Media as Positive Influences

## How Music Affects Your Teen's Life

I am personally a big fan of great music, but I believe that in our society teens are subject to destructive messages of violence, hate, fear, killing and sex from the music they listen to. Record companies make billions of dollars because our youth buy these records filled with negative messages. Music affects your teenager because listening to it builds a belief system, resulting in behaviors that mirror the messages they hear in music. Music instills values in our youth; at a young age children will model the behaviors of what they hear and see in music videos. Some professional musicians are experts at building a false sense of rapport with teens.

I was told all my life by my parents that I should not listen to certain types of music. At that time, I thought my parents were old-fashioned and simply did not know what they were talking about. After acquiring some maturity and being in this field for over seventeen years, I realized that my parents were right. What you listen to, you become.

Music has shaped our destiny in both positive and negative ways. I feel that certain forms of music can make our teens achieve greatness and other forms can limit their potentials. Music is a powerful tool, one that can create a belief system. For instance, if a teen listens to music and repeats the words with feeling and emotions, it can condition their mind and build a belief system. For instance, the song "Don't Worry, Be Happy" sold millions of records with its positive messages that people still quote today.

If you say something negative to your child every day, soon they will believe what you are saying. Our brain picks up music unconsciously and processes music in the following fashion:

- Words = 7%
- Tone, Tempo Tonality =38%
- Body Movement =55%.

Most songs that make it on the top of the music lists are what I call a VAK, meaning the lyrics have **visual** meaning (a fast beat to dance to) and **auditory** tone, tempo and tonality. Most of these songs are also **kinesthetic,** meaning they appeal to the physical nature of a child, including their feelings and emotions. Using all three methods of communication, music effectively builds a subconscious bond between our teens in professional musicians. All of these factors shape their belief systems and form their values of the world.

If we use music with lyrics that is on the top of the chart/VAK and teens start moving their bodies with dance movements, they become ripe for brain conditioning (most learning theorists state that body states can make one highly suggestible to classically conditioned learning). For example, with the classic study of Pavlov's dog, a bell is rung and the dog salivates. Every time the dog hears the bell, the dog wants to eat. The same is true when our youth hear certain music; they respond like Pavlov's dog.

Consequently, if the music sends a negative message while children are in this state, they will have strong desires to mimic the attitudes and behaviors expressed in the music. This could be why music gains rapport with our teens. The teens see the artist and the band members and they relate to them. The band members use just the right words, tone and physiology. The rhythms mirror physiology and can stimulate the brain and the autonomic nervous system. The lyrics identify common youthful feelings and angst. The artist gains trust and loyalty from teens, and then the teens build a bond with the musician. The process of moving one's body with feelings and emotions influences the brain, and subsequently behaviors. Saying something with feeling and emotions while emphasizing those works with movement is referred to as *incantation.* This can be done in a negative or positive way.

So when music artists talk about killing, sex and violence in their songs, and then your teen sings along with the music with feeling—his or her emotions "feed" the subconscious mind and create a belief. A belief is a feeling of certainty. Therefore, if your teen feels what the artist says is true, or the musician's actions on the video look appealing and it matches how they want to behave–the combined impact will make their actions fit what the artist is modeling.

**Action Plan for Parents Around Music/Media Influences**

**Use principal five**: Engage your teens in conversation. Find out what music they listen to and who their favorite musicians are. Once these questions are answered, research the musicians and type of music. This means you must research what messages the artist or group is sending to your child. You should also actually listen to your child music of choice with them and express an interest. Then you can see first hand if your child is listening to negative or positive music.

**Case Example**

In my private practice, I worked with a teen, Tina, who listened to hard rock music. I asked Tina if she would bring in a CD so I could listen to it. She appeared very happy that I would take the time to listen to her music. Her goal was to earn good grades in school. I explained to her that my job as a coach was to help her achieve her goals, and since her grades had dropped in the last six months, I wanted to find out why.

During our next meeting, Tina let me listen to her music and I was immediately able to determine why her grades had been dropping and why she changed her style of dress. The lyrics were negative, if not destructive. When I asked her why she started listening to this music, she told me that her friends introduced her to this band. I asked her to define anew what her future goals in life would be, and when she told me to be a nurse and to help people, I knew she needed some assistance. I told her that I admired her goal of becoming a nurse, but that nurses needed to earn a certain GPA to get into school, and with her grades slipping, and her behavior changing this might not take place. I explained to Tina the consequences of not having good grades and the possible costs if she did reach her goals. I informed her that she would become the music that she listened to and would become like the people that she hung out with. I also told her that sometimes people lower their standards just to have friends accept them.

Then I explained the benefits of improving her grades and listening to music that would be positive in her life. Choosing new friends could help to raise her standards and reach her goals. I emphasized that only she could make these decisions, but that I hoped she would make the right choices. After about a month, she took my speech to heart and made the necessary changes in her life.  Today, Tina is a psychiatric nurse in the Midwest helping youth with emotional challenges.

## The Need to Bond the Family Together

Now you are ready to put all the information you have learned together to create the family that you deserve. People must put the same energy into their families as they do into the other aspects of their lives. Too many people are addicted to the Internet, television and video games. Depression and violence are rampant in our society, and teen suicide is also at an all time high. How can we reclaim our teenagers?

Parents have the responsibility to be friendly to their children, but not their friends. In my private practice, I have seen many cases where the teenagers were being the parents and the parents were being their children's friends. This cannot take place if you want to build a strong, respectful relationship with your child. Boundaries must be established.

For instance, I worked with a fifteen-year-old teen in my private practice who appeared on the outside to be fine since he was doing exceptionally well in school. After three months of working with him, he stopped coming to see me, feeling it was time for him to move on and utilize the tools he had learned in counseling. After awhile, his grades began to decline and he began to mistreat his parents. He finally returned to see me, admitting he was sexually active with several different girls. He had told his mother since she asked for complete honesty, but it had resulted in a big argument over whether he could have his girlfriend over to the house. His mother did not want to anger him so she allowed him to have his way. He invited three of his girlfriends over to spend the night.

The teenagers watched television for a long while and the mother tried to stay up with them as late as possible, but eventually she went to sleep. The young man and his girlfriends went into this bedroom to drink and 'have fun.' The teen boy had sex with one of the females in his bedrooms right in his parent's home.

The mother wanted to be friends with her son instead of being a parent to him. This cost her respect from her peers, specifically the parents of the three girls. This also cost her respect from her son. Parents must establish consistent boundaries with their teenagers and enforce those boundaries.

Parents need to also make it a point to meet their children's friends and their parents. By meeting the parents of your teenager's friends, you can get a good idea of the friends' values and attitudes. For example, if a teen is on a diet and some of his/her friends are eating cake, they may pressure the teen into having a piece too. Much of the time, a teenager will do what their friends are doing to show his/her love and solidarity for them. A teenager may do something to just feel part of the group, what most people term as "peer pressure." So the teen on the diet may eat the piece of cake, going against his/her goal to be healthy, and then after eating the cake, will feel badly. This teen would be more successful if he/she associated with others that took care of their bodies and respected his/her goals for a healthier lifestyle.

Choosing good friends over bad simply means that teenagers choose friends that reinforce their values, not someone who tears them down. This choice is deliberate and may require help with clarification of values. Teenagers must learn to raise their standards, stick with those standards and associate with friends that strengthen their values. For example, when people enter into the Marines, they are met with an environment that challenges them to be their very best. They are able to accomplish tasks they may not have believed before that they could do. When they go back home and hang out with old friends, however, they tend to lower their standards, such as allowing themselves to get out of shape.

Challenge your teenager to be the best he/she can be. A person's physical condition has much to do with how he/she will function emotionally and socially. To be at their best mentally children must be physically fit. Obesity is at an all-time high in this country, along with stress related diseases. Teenagers often have illusions of immortality, believing that the health choices they make now will not matter later.

When I was growing up, my friends and I always were active, playing basketball, football and hanging out at the Boys and Girls Club, which has a variety of physical activities. In the 21$^{st}$ century, children's activities are much more sedentary, involving watching hours of television, whittling away time on the Internet and playing video games. A study was conducted three years ago that revealed one out of every three teenagers is obese. Out of the 50 states, only one state requires teenagers to pass a physical fitness test to graduate from high school. Parents must be responsible for motivating their teens to work out and eat healthy foods.

In my private practice, I worked with an obese teenager who was constantly teased at school, referred to by his peers as "Piggy." What do you think the outcome of his life will be? This young man grew up with low self-worth until he lost the weight. Once he got into better shape, he began to like himself and his behavior in all aspects positively changed.

Physical and psychological challenges such as self-esteem, depression and other negative behaviors can surface during the teenage years. To help cope and relieve these challenges, teens should participate in any sort of physical activity, whether an exercise program or chores around the house. Even better, families could establish a family exercise routine that helps everyone reach a state of fitness. Of course, those with health issues should consult their physician before beginning an exercise program.

Turn off the television, cancel the Internet and hide the video games to get your teenagers to get out and move. Model good physical fitness and teach your children how exercise and physical recreation can be a powerful stress management tool.

## The Mental Challenge: Are You Ready to Bond?

Now that you have realized the importance of connecting with your children, you realize that it is easy. Start now by practicing what you have learned from this book. Take on the 'Ten-Day Mental Challenge' by focusing on these principles you have learned over the next ten days with your teenagers and see how they will significantly change your lives. Do not stop there, but continue to utilize these principles again and again. You will feel more love for your teenager and they will love you for it!

My goal is to give you enough information to help you achieve a strong bond with your child. I know that is you can connect with your children on a conscious and unconscious level, and then your family's lives will positively transform.

Dare to make your life magnificent!

Love and Peace,

Dr. John Oda

# Special Addenda:  Case Summary

What follows are summaries (also called case studies) of some of my cases. My goal is to help you, the parents or caregivers of teens, to understand and work with your teenagers. This selective case summary embodies the utilization of the **Seven Principles** that I have already covered.  To ensure confidentiality, I have changed some of the facts of the case, such as names, while preserving the core issues that the parents and I dealt with in treatment.

In working with others, I have had the honor of meeting many teenagers throughout my career.  Several cases readily stand out in my mind that would be helpful to share.  In my work, I have discovered that some of the lives I have touched have also changed my life as a therapist.  My hope is that these case summaries will provide parents with valuable insights about how to deal with their teenagers.  Finally, by reading these cases and using the **Seven Principles**, together we can prevent some of the negative outcomes depicted here from ever happening to your family.

### Case One

In the early part of my career, I counseled a "gifted" teenager named Jacob. He was an all-state football player, and academically, his grades were above average.  At the time of his admission, he seemed to have his head on his shoulders and his family seemed very supportive of his athletic and academic abilities, helping him with the process of choosing a college.

I soon found out, however, that Jacob had a history with many challenges.  He was eaten up with anger, depression, had recently discovered school challenges, and was using drugs.  Jacob's parents were an upper-middle-class family that had high hopes for Jacob's future.  Jacob had been a relatively average teen, doing well in school and playing a sport that he had loved since the third grade.  Starting in the ninth grade, Jacob's parents noticed that his grades were slipping and sought advice from one of their friends who happened to be a schoolteacher.

*His parents did not teach Jacob the first technique:  Teach something of value to your teenager, and then instill a sense of reason and purpose.*

This teacher told Jacob's parents that he would speak with Jacob about the importance of earning good grades. This man had a talk with Jacob, and his grades subsequently improved. At the end of the same school year, numerous colleges contacted Jacob about playing football for them in the future. Things again seemed to be going well for Jacob.

In his junior year of high school, his parents began to notice that they did not have much interaction with Jacob, though his grades were much better and everything seemed fine. If they wanted a report about how Jacob was doing they would talk to their friend, the teacher. But the parents noticed a great deal of anger in Jacob, and when they would ask him what was wrong, he would snap at them. Again, his grades began to slip, and he was even skipping school, and missing football practice. Jacob's parents were puzzled, because he had always demonstrated a passion for this sport, and had never missed practice for any reason.

*In this situation, Jacob's parents could have used the principle Two, of finding one activity to participate in with their teenager to connect with their son.*

One day, while cleaning his room, Jacob's parents found some cocaine, but were too timid to confront him about it, so they asked their teacher-friend to talk to him. Jacob denied that the cocaine was his, and told his parents that it belonged to a friend. His parents gave him the benefit of the doubt. Later that year, Jacob quit football altogether and was flunking his classes. He told his parents he wanted to quit school. His parents began to blame themselves for Jacob's attitude and actions.

*Another principle Five, Jacob's parents could have used to connect with Jacob is to engage your teen in conversation.*

A crucial error occurred when Jacob's parents were afraid to confront him and had someone else do that instead. There is no substitution for a parent in regards to taking an active interest in their teenager. For example, his parents could have encouraged communication by asking open questions such as, "What are your favorite classes?" "Are you having fun in football?" "What happened to your friend Jim, we haven't seen him around the house?" Instead, his parents had an old family friend speak with Jacob. They saw this friend of twenty years as a trusted expert; however, experts cannot substitute the responsibility parents have for establishing communication and a loving home environment for the teenagers.

Still, their teacher friend continued to offer his expertise about Jacob's situation, saying that Jacob was just going through some problems at school, and that he would be willing to talk to him again. Jacob's parents told him to go to the teacher's house, but Jacob adamantly stated that he did not want to go. Despite this, Jacob's parents forced him to see the teacher because they did not know how to communicate with Jacob.

*In this situation, Jacob's parents could have simply used Principle Six, tell your child that you love him/her.*

As it turned out, there was a very valid reason that Jacob did not want to see this friend of his parents, but Jacob did not know how to communicate this to his parents. This trusted friend of the parents was actually supplying Jacob with drugs for the past two years, including LSD and cocaine. When Jacob would pass out, or be otherwise incapacitated, the teacher would sexually assault Jacob. At times, Jacob would wake up in the middle of this, but continue to fake like he was passed out, out of fear. Jacob was terrified and ashamed, because he was repeatedly being molested by a so-called "family friend." He did not know how to tell this to his parents, because the teacher was such a close friend. As a result, Jacob became full of rage, and his drug use increased.

*If Jacob's parents had discovered this before he came to the hospital, they might have been able to restore a sense of order to their son's life. There is perhaps only one principle to be used in the face of such extreme urgency; Principle Seven, to have an attitude of gratitude. This principle can be used as a catalyst for a new beginning and allow the healing process to begin.*

After Jacob arrived at the hospital where I worked, he was very angry with the world. He completely lacked trust for anyone, and did not smile at all that first week. One of Jacob's triggers (an unintentional recall of past abuse in the present) was any man wearing a tie, since the teacher always wore a tie. This made my job a bit challenging, because one of our unit's social workers always wore a tie. I asked this coworker to not wear a tie around Jacob, but he did not listen.

One day, this social worker was working around Jacob, and Jacob had a sudden flashback (this can occur in post-traumatic cases). In a fit of rage, Jacob tried to attack the social worker. Keep in mind that Jacob was about 220 pounds, while the social worker weighed only 140 pounds. The hospital staff called a code green, which meant they were dealing with a violent client. When I arrived, they had about ten men holding down Jacob, with Jacob fighting the entire time. From his verbalizations and other cues, it appeared that Jacob had regressed to a moment when the teacher was assaulting him. Jacob was yelling, "Get off of me! I'm going to kill you!" along with other expletives. I asked Jacob what today's date was, and the date he provided was about three months earlier. I told the other staff that I would take the lead in approaching Jacob.

After about twenty minutes, I was able to calm him down, while the rest of the team prepared to take Jacob to the "quiet room." This was the usual procedure after such an incident with one of the teenagers, but this time, things would be a bit different. Most of the time, we would put a teen in restraints under these circumstances. With Jacob, I did not use restraints, but directed him to get up and walk to the "quiet room" by himself. The staff seemed amazed about what had happened, but this represented a crucial opportunity for Jacob to make, what would eventually be, a breakthrough. It was also the beginning of a great rapport between Jacob and me.

Eventually, I was able to work with Jacob in helping diffuse his triggers and deal with the impact of his abuse. In short, I taught Jacob some of the tools that I have shared with you in this book. Jacob stayed in the hospital for about twelve months, learning techniques to help him deal with his drug use, anger and rage, history of being molested and his various self-esteem issues. Although he improved and returned home, he never went to college to play football.

**Case Two**

In my private practice I work with many teens or pre-teens who are faced with multiple challenges. One case that especially baffled me was with a ten-year-old pre-teen, 'Keith,' who had missed **45 days** of school. His mother told me that she tried everything with him. His mother took him to school but he would fight her every day about attending. His mother put him on punishment, took away his toys, had the pastor speak to him, the police speak to him, yet nothing worked.

Eventually his mother, Beth, brought Keith to my office. He seemed rather big for his age, and Beth appeared worn out trying to find a way to work with her son. After our first meeting, I told Beth that by the fall her son would be going to school.

*Beth did not use principle one:   teaching Keith something of value and finding a reason or purpose.*

In spite of my optimism, Beth did not have to say anything to me; her body language said it all. She did not seem to believe in me. I told her that we would be doing groups with preteens his same age, utilizing individual therapy and family sessions. These sessions would occur once a week for quite a while, and then in six months, Keith would not need to see me anymore. Beth felt hopeless which hindered her ability to implement principles that I would be teaching her from the seven principles. Such hopelessness also impacted her ability to focus.

Time and again, I have seen cases like this where just a little bit of light, just a small hopeful beginning, if perceived by the parent, can capitalize into utter dismissal of hopelessness and the blossoming of full blown hope. As such parents begin to believe in the power of the seven principles to change their children, we can see a full reversal of what educators have termed the Pygmalion Effect. That is, as the parents begin to believe in the child, even in small ways, then the child too begins to believe in him or herself and begins to challenge negative labels that have been consciously and unconsciously attached to his behaviors and often uncritically to his sense of self. The effect of hope is a counter effect that begins to reverse this destructive process.

I have worked in this field for so long that I know the length of time it will take me to get the results that I am seeking with a teen. That is why I knew what to say to Beth to begin to instill a sense of hope. That first meeting with Keith seemed a bit contrary to expectations as he seemed to be very "normal." For example, he understood the importance of going to school, and what the consequences of not going to school could bring. He told me that his pastor and family's friends had all spoken to him several times about going to school. My first approach was to put fear in his heart, to explain to him that if he did not change his pattern of missing school, he would be sent to a residential placement or foster home until the age of 18. That approach did not work because Beth was not on the same page and it appeared that she treated Keith like a baby and spoiled him.

My second approach was having a meeting with Beth to find out what was taking place at home and why Keith did not want go to school. Beth told me that Keith stayed with his Aunt during the day because she worked. Beth reported that many times the Aunt attempted to take Keith to school, but he resisted her efforts as well. She said many times Keith had struck her and had thrown things at other family members. Beth appeared to be frightened of Keith's ten-year-old temper. It left me wondering, 'Who was in control here?'

*Beth also did not use the second principle: Find one thing to do with your preteen.*

I explained to Beth that we would work together on his temper, his rage and developing respect for his mother and family. After the meeting, I wanted to have a family session with the entire family to find out what was going on at home. The signs of trouble were dominant since something did not seem right. Why would a ten-year-old child want to stay home and not attend school?

I met his family, including his aunt. His aunt, or rather, great aunt, seemed to be about ninety years old, as she looked very elderly and fragile, about 90 pounds. They had to help her to my office and Keith seemed to appear very worried about her. The great aunt looked like she could be carried away by the wind at any moment! Now, I was truly curious. I asked the family about what was going on at home that kept Keith from missing school. The great aunt said when Keith came to her house, he did not want to go to school and he regularly went back to bed. When he woke up, she reported that Keith played video games all day. Can you see how rewarding it was for Keith to stay home at the great aunt's?

*Beth might have used principle three: Parents should do something for their preteens, nothing material. Beth would buy Keith video games, expensive clothes, because she did not want him to get upset with her.*

To make the experience of staying home less pleasant, I explained to the family when Keith was not in school that he needed to do chores and his homework. Beth and the great aunt seemed very confused about that notion. Then when I asked Keith directly as to why he wanted to stay home, he said he wanted to take care of his great aunt. I asked him why he wanted to take care of his great aunt, and Keith stated: "My mother told me she's going to die soon, and since she's at work, no one can take care of her." Now it was obvious as to what was going on here. Keith felt like he had to take care of his great aunt. This was clearly an awesome and overwhelming responsibility for a ten-year-old to take on. It was certainly age inappropriate, but it was based in genuine love and caring. It appeared that in Keith's mind, he associated staying home with his great aunt as meaning that he could protect her and keep her from dying. After a couple more sessions with the family, I realized my plan of action.

***Beth did not use the fifth principle: Ask your preteen for conversation. For example, the crucial question for Keith, "why do you like staying home from school?" Of course not knowing what was happening in his mind before asking, she might have asked these additional questions that address school avoidance: 'Do you like school? Who's your favorite teacher? Does anyone pick on you at school?"***

I invited Keith to attend group with other preteens his own age. I realized that I needed to create some sense of leverage with him, meaning I needed to create a lot of 'pain' for not going to school. I would use the group to provide both peer support and peer pressure to help him gain some insight about his behavior. I also hoped the group would let him know that even though he might have good intentions for his great aunt, this may have just been an excuse for his behavior.

When the group around the room stated why they were there, Keith smiled and said, "I missed 45 days of school." Some of his peers in the group appeared very shocked. It was a complete surprise to the rest of the group that someone their age would miss so much school. When some of the teens asked him why he had missed so much school, his response was, "I just did not want to go."

His peers began to create the pain that he needed in order to make changes and they explained to him what it would cost him in the near future. They described possible outcomes such as troubles with his parents, conflicts with other authority figures and academic failures. Then, since other parents also attended the group, some of the parents explained to Beth that she needed to take more responsibility as a mother, as well as the responsibility to make sure the great aunt's needs were met, so that Keith would have neither the excuse or need to care for her.

After the first group session where we worked with Keith, the desired outcome was ascertained. I did not see him for about ten days, and when he returned to group it was evident that he had been thinking about what the group advised previously. At the second group, there were also other parents in attendance. We decided to do role plays where I deliberately gave Keith one of the parents who was very direct with their pre-teen. Consequently, I had Sue play Keith's mother and had Beth observe, so that she could see how other parents would handle her challenge. This way, she would reap the benefits of having healthy, alternative ways of addressing this concern being modeled for her.

Sue did not accept any of Keith's excuse making, explaining to him the rules of the house. Sue directly stated: "I go to work everyday, I expect you to attend school daily." Sue explained to Keith if he missed school, he would not be allowed play at his friends' houses, play video games or have any fun activities. Sue then asked Keith some magnificent questions: "What benefits would you get from going to school? How would that affect your life in the future?" Sue then had Keith stop, really focus and politely demanded that he answer the questions. After he identified both the negative results of not going to school and the positive benefits of going to school, Keith now felt pain for not going, and pleasure for going to school in the fall. Sue also told him that he could only miss four days of school from then on.

The third and next session would tackle the task of showing him how to interrupt his own limited pattern. As a way to understand this technique for creating change, think about when you may have been talking with a friend and someone interrupted you so that you forgot what you were saying. When this happens in therapy, it is referred to as a pattern interruption. I needed to show Keith how to interrupt his own patterns.

I explained to the entire group that we would do something called the board break. My goal was to show them how to break through their fears and limitations by anchoring these abstractions into a concrete act. We would basically be constructing a metaphor for 'breaking through' perceived challenges. I explained to them how powerful the brain is and showed them through many examples about how to tap into their potentials. Once this was done, I retrieved the pine boards, measuring 8 1/2 inches by 11 inches, and explained how they would break the board with simple karate techniques. In doing this, I planned to show them ways to take control of their lives. They would do this by moving their bodies a different way and changing the way they speak to themselves.

At that point, Keith flat out told me that he could not break the board. I told Keith that he first needed to identify a target, so he wrote on the front part of the board "missing 45 days of school." I directed him to consider what he wanted instead of the target and to write this on the backside of the board. He wrote, "to miss 4 days of school." He had just mapped out a change in his belief system. After instruction in the technique that changed his belief system, Keith actually broke through the board. From that day on, he changed his beliefs about school.

The fourth session was an individual session where I had to condition his new behavior. To do this, we played his favorite music and I coached him in exercises where he visualized himself going to school and getting excellent grades. Then I had him yelling without emotions, positive statements about him going to school and getting positive results. We danced for about 45 minutes, until we conditioned it in his brain and it became a habit. After the session, I showed him how to reward himself, by patting himself on the back when he does something close to right, telling Keith that this will build up the nervous system. He could then condition his own behaviors anytime he wanted to and produce results anytime he must do so.

We met throughout the summer for a total of about ten times. The last time I spoke with his mother, Beth, she stated that he was getting outstanding grades, had missed only three days of school and only had a month of school left. This case is a strong example of what can happen when all we have to do is change our mindsets and our beliefs, producing wonderful results.

**Case Three**

Many cases have shaped the quality of my life, and some have stayed with me because of the amazing ability of the human spirit to transcend difficulties and to ultimately triumph. Some people continue to amaze me with their willingness to overcome their challenges. 'Heather' is one of these cases. Early in my clinical career, I met this young woman. It appeared that she had many challenges in her life. In the past, she had tried several times to commit suicide and luckily, was unable to find a lethal way. She used to cut on her wrists believing that no one loved her. Her parents had tried numerous counselors and nothing had helped. They wanted the best for their child, but did not know how to communicate with her. One night, Heather got angry with her parents and she wanted to end her life. Heather took an excess of pills (overdose is the leading cause of suicide among females), and her parents later found her, so they took her to the emergency room. After pumping her stomach, she was transferred to the hospital where I was on duty.

My goal as her therapist would be to give her some new tools, such as helping her believe in herself by loving herself and rebuilding her self-esteem. I knew that I had a big challenge ahead of me, and since my goal is to always give every client whatever they need, I would do my very best to show Heather the easiest way to obtain the best results and outcomes that were needed.

During Heather's first three days in the hospital, she slept all day. She had very little interaction with peers and staff. Since Heather was on my caseload, this meant that I had to come up with a treatment plan and work with her. No matter what, I resolved to do my very best to communicate this to her and help her. Teens and everyone else do need to know that the challenges they are facing can be handled. Good caregivers must communicate this because it instills a strong sense of coping and hope. So, on the fourth day, I was surprised when Heather came out of her room. She was very angry with the dayshift staff. In fact, on repeated days thereafter, she would go into restraints fighting and kicking for her dear life. They would have her on lockdown status, meaning that she was in a quiet room, with the door locked and padded walls. Heather would yell, scream and kick until she passed out from exhaustion. I knew immediately that she must have a strong will and that underneath all of her troubles was some strong ego strength. Now if I could just help her to harness it and focus it. After she and I began to connect, she would not be put into restraints during my shift, which was the evening shift.

In groups, Heather would talk about wanting to end her life. She also talked about not connecting with her parents and how her parents would not let her be a teenager. Consequently, I asked Heather what would have to happen for her to become a teenager and what her parents would have to do. Heather appeared very puzzled, and said nothing since she said she had never thought about that before.

During our individual sessions, I began to explain to her that changes happen in a moment. I also pointed out to her that it seemed like she wanted to be in this space with all the anger and depression. That is, that she must be getting something out of it. At that point, Heather stated, "I don't want to be like this anymore! I've tried everything, how can you help me?" The honest and articulated cry for help borne out of exasperation is often the beginning of a significant moment in anyone's therapy, so I leapt at the opportunity.

Since I was Heather's therapist and one of my personal outcomes would be simply to challenge her, I told her it would only take me five days to help her. I also explained to Heather that if she wanted my help, she must want to change; it must be a burning desire and it must provide a new purpose to live. So when we ended our session, Heather seemed very confused and did not know what to say about our conversation.

The following day, according to the dayshift's report, Heather did not go into restraints, but rather had a great day and wanted to learn about moving up to the next level. Her attitude seemed to change overnight. When I arrived at work, Heather told me that she had some bad news. Heather stated, "I have been here for three weeks, and haven't worked on my problems, and now, I only have one week left before my insurance runs out." Again, I changed her belief system about making a powerful change in only five days. Creating expectancies that something positive is going to happen helps them to happen. The other part would be to encourage Heather to adopt new ways of behaving that would help her to meet her needs and harness that great will within her.

I told Heather we needed to begin our collaborative journey NOW! I emphasized that we only had five days because I was off on the weekend, which helped to create a sense of urgency. This would bring home the notion that there would be some finality and completeness to the work that we would be doing. Not only did I tell her we would do the work in five days, I also told her how we would do it and where we would start.

Since I told Heather that we would be taking one step at a time, I explained to her that we needed to work on her self-esteem first. To do this, I had her write 40 positive things about herself each day. I also explained to her that she needed to look in the mirror and say, "I love all of me" with feelings and emotions so it would become conditioned into her subconscious mind, her demeanor, and become part of her belief system. Heather gave me a look (one of those dubious looks that people have) and then she stated that she did not love herself at all. I told her that we could work on that, so I had her begin to say out loud, "I like all of me" ten times in the morning and ten times at night. As Heather's counselor, I felt it was my duty to push her, and if she did not complete the homework, I knew it likely meant that she really did not want to change.

During our next individual session, I talked about the possibilities of change, how it would look, hear and feel. I reminded her that she needed to have some urgency on making a change NOW! The next day she had written down 50 positive things about herself and had looked in the mirror and stated "I like all of me." I then told her to hang her positive statements up on her bedroom wall so that if she had a bad hour she could take a look at them. I told her to adopt the belief that she can never have a bad day, but maybe only a bad hour or minute. In describing that she would 'never have a bad day', my goal was to teach her tools that she could use to change her mental and emotional state, make her focus on what she wanted in life and how to get it. She would do this by focusing on the positive things about herself, changing her beliefs, handling whatever life threw her way and definitely not by merely looking at her circumstances.

For the next five days, the team and I did many interventions and explored ways of working on her anger, self-esteem, depression and self-cutting. After those five days where we concentrated on showing her how she functions as a human, with her help, we co-discovered what triggered her and identified and modified her irrational "rules." We began to see a new Heather emerge. Then, when we worked on how she processed information and gave her tools to deal with past abuse, Heather was ready for graduation. Heather and the entire team had come up with a system that could truly help her. Later, when her parents came to the hospital they noticed an immediate change in her behavior. Her parents appeared very happy and provided assistance for Heather to go to a residential treatment center for fifteen days where she continued to work on her issues (in most cases teens would go to residential treatment for the average of one year). Heather is no longer self-mutilating, she loves herself and she is getting along with her family.

**A letter from Heather after she left the hospital:**

Dear John,

Thank you, Thank you, for being born. Thank you for loving your job. Thank you for loving yourself. And thank you for helping me. Those compliments that I made to you last night were true: and I mean them from the bottom of my heart. When I first met you, I liked you. I did not have to go through hating you to get to liking you. You are *Phenomenal! Outstanding*! And you know it!

Before I came here, I did not believe that I could get better! I thought just accept it and let me die, but now, because of coming here and doing all the work I have done, I now want to live! So I will be calling you and talking to you later, Mr. John.

Sincerely and gratefully,

Heather

**Case Four**

Angela was a fourteen-year-old female living with her mother and her mother's boyfriend. Angela had a voice like an angel and had always wanted to become a singer. When I first met her, Angela seemed to have anger and lacked trust for men. Her mother did not bother to verbally and affectionately communicate with Angela. Instead Angela's mother was always yelling, hitting and throwing things at her. This is not the kind of communication that teens need!

Angela believed that her mother did not love her so she attempted to kill herself by taking pills. She arrived at the hospital and appeared very angry at the world. She was likely really angry at her mom and due to Angela's issues,

45

it was likely she had been mistreated or abused by men. Angela ended up on my patient load and our first interactions were not the best. She refused to attend any groups as she only wanted to stay in bed. Since I have always believed in trying my hardest to meet the patient's needs, I brought the groups to Angela. For quite awhile, she would say very colorful things to me, that is, she cursed me out. After about ten days of going through this, she finally came out of her room to attend one of my groups. After about ten minutes she left the room, stating, "I'm not going to a man's group again."

I went to her room with a female staff member to see if she was all right. Of course she said some very rude things, so I sent her to the 'Quiet Room.' I explained to her that I was not sure how she talked to her parents, but I demanded respect, and that meant that no one spoke to me like she had. After spending two hours in the Quiet Room, her attitude changed. When she got out of the Quiet Room, we actually had our first conversation. It started because I practiced my **fifth** principle—I simply asked her for some conversation. We talked about her school and her hobbies. When Angela talked about becoming a singer, I asked her if she could sing for me. Angela told me that she was too embarrassed, but I reassured her that she would be able to do so in due time.

The next day Angela appeared to be very happy. I asked her about her parents, noticing she did not want to talk about her mother but seemed happy while talking about her father. I asked Angela if she felt her parents loved her. At that question, Angela paused and stated, "I don't know." Apparently, her parents had not used **principle six: tell your child that you love them.** (At least if they had, she could not remember it, it was too long ago to remember, or it was not memorable). I explained to Angela that I wanted to help her realize that she was a special person. Angela asked me what she had to give me if I helped her. I explained to Angela I only wanted her to give me 100%, meaning allow me to be her therapist and work out her challenges. I simply told her that I was not going to hurt her and that my only goal was to help her accomplish her goals in life. Angela appeared very puzzled at this point since all of her life everyone had been taking advantage of her, meaning she had suffered numerous abuses--mental, physical and sexual abuses. To trust, to believe that anyone, especially a man, would truly and genuinely want to help her was a totally new concept to her. She would have to take a risk to learn something new, but for now, she wanted to know what angle I was coming from.

First, I asked Angela what she wanted to get out of treatment; that is, what did she want help with. When she replied she did not know what she wanted, I explained that the purpose of getting better would become plain to her as we talked and worked on her issues. I reassured her **we would stop here with her treatment.** The way to benefit from her problems would be to 'get everything out'; there was no substitute for talking about what was bothering her, and this was a safe place to do it. I told her that she would have to deal with her challenges. I then explained to her the reasons for dealing with them now, instead of ten years from now. With Angela, I utilized my **first principle: Teach something of value to your teen, and then help them to have a reason or a purpose.**

In our next one-on-one session, I asked Angela to explain why she tried to kill herself. She revealed to me that her mother's boyfriend had raped her. When Angela told her mother, she had not believed her. In fact, her mother had called her a liar. Angela told her mother that she was a virgin and would never lie about that. I explained to Angela that our very next session together would be a family session where we would confront her mother, Ruth, and her mother's boyfriend about what took place. When Angela stated, "I'm too scared to confront my mother, she might hit me," I explained to Angela that staff would be present and that we would not allow anything to happen to her.

The family session happened the very next day, but the boyfriend was unable to attend. Angela appeared to be very scared and nervous. I explained to everyone the rules for this type of sessions; namely, about respecting everyone, no yelling, screaming and no getting up to leave until staff excused the person. I also reassured everyone that they would have a chance to speak. Angela had written everything down that she wanted to say on a piece of paper. Also, before the family session Angela and I role-played everything that could possibly go wrong in her session to get her ready for anything.

I had Angela speak first, just after I instructed Ruth to give Angela time to talk and to please not interrupt her until she was completely finished. Angela explained the abuse that was going on in the house, about how her mother's boyfriend had raped her and how her mother's siding with him had upset her and hurt her feelings. Ruth listened, and although she appeared to be very upset, she respected what Angela had to say. Finally, after Angela talked about what took place Ruth exclaimed, "I don't know why anyone would want my daughter, especially my boyfriend!"

At that point, tears flowed out of Angela's eyes, but then strength and rage seemed to emerge from within her, from deep within her, a part of her that had never been seen before. The drama was evident, as now perhaps for the first time, this young woman was utterly and fully able to express herself in dialogue to her mother and actually have her mother listen to her. Angela stated that the mother's boyfriend had a tattoo, which she described in vivid detail, and that this tattoo was only visible if he were nude. When Angela told her mother about the boyfriend's tattoo, tears came to Ruth's eyes, as she realized her daughter was telling the truth. She reached out to her daughter then for a hug, and while she gave her daughter a hug, she stated her sorrow for not believing her. Angela appeared to be happy, as it seemed her mother had finally believed her for the first time. That family session ended on a wonderful note.

That same day Angela and I talked about what happened. Angela was so excited and started planning her life with her mother. I had a gut feeling that something was not right and told her that she needed to focus on the moment. I wanted her to build on this victory, not to rest in it. I knew that she still needed to work on her treatment issues and I did not want her to lose sight of that even though Angela seemed to really connect with her mother. I did not want Angela's treatment to become Angela *and* her mother's treatment at this point, because Angela still had some important issues to resolve. I knew she would only be able to respond to her mother's needs in these family issues after she worked on herself. I also knew that children cannot take on their parents' issues because it robs them of taking care of their needs and can prevent parents from becoming 'adult enough' to work on their own issues responsibly. Many years of experience have taught me time and again: that after teens have bonded with their parents through some trauma, they can love their parents so much that they can forget to work on themselves—and the changes are therefore not able to really deepen. My task was to tell Angela in every way possible, "Angela, at this time, you and I need to take this victory and work on your treatment, not your mother's."

The next day Ruth called and wanted to meet again, but the boyfriend wanted to be present this time. I told her mother that I needed to ask Angela if she wanted to have him in the meeting. When Angela replied that she would consent for the mother's boyfriend to be present, I explained to Angela the possibility that her mother might appear to 'change sides' due to the mother already having a relationship with the boyfriend. I also cautioned Angela that the boyfriend might deny everything. By doing so, I attempted to prepare her for everything that could take place.

The day of the next family meeting, it was a tense atmosphere, with both the boyfriend and Angela's mother being present. I could not explain why, but my gut told me that something was wrong. I had a terrible feeling that the session would not go the way Angela wanted it to go. Again, I explained to everyone the rules of the family session. Everyone agreed that they would hold themselves to that standard. When we began the session, Ruth wanted to talk first. She described confronting her boyfriend, and she stated that he told her that Angela wanted him to have sex with her. Angela began to cry, and stated that this was not true (it had not occurred to Ruth that sex between the boyfriend and her daughter was sex abuse no matter what since Angela was a minor). I told Angela that her mother had the floor and we needed to let her finish what she was saying.

Ruth explained that her boyfriend was thirty-four years old and that he could not have helped himself because Angela would wear tank tops and shorts around him. She reasoned that because it made him think of sex, it was acceptable for him to have sex with Angela. Basically, Ruth was playing the victim. Further, Ruth told us that since Angela had slept with her boyfriend, that Angela was no longer welcome in their house. She also stated that she would give up custody of Angela, allowing her ex-husband to have custody of her, because she believed her daughter was a slut.

At that point, I jumped in, telling Ruth her views were totally inappropriate, that name-calling would not be tolerated in this session and that she needed to respect Angela's feelings and hear what had really happened. Angela started crying and I asked her to leave the session as I needed to speak further with her mother and the boyfriend. I asked another staff member to sit in with me.

I then reprimanded Ruth for being so rude and disrespectful to her child. I told the mother that she is justifying and making excuses for her boyfriend's sick behavior and wrongfully blaming her own daughter for what he had done to her. I explained to Ruth that I was going to file charges against her boyfriend, and I did not want her to come back to the hospital. I let Ruth know that as a mother, she was supposed to love her child, yet she was not helping Angela at all. Finally, (and I admit it) in exasperation, I stated, "It appears that you believe your boyfriend of one year over your own daughter.

How could you be with a man that raped your daughter?" I then told them both that the family session was over and that they needed to leave the hospital immediately.

Afterwards, I spoke to Angela about what had happened and we identified her thoughts and feelings. Understandably, Angela appeared very upset and had a difficult time processing what took place. After spending some time with her, I told Angela that she needed to think about things and to be away from distractions, so I suggested that she go to the Quiet Room. Also, I wanted her there so staff could watch her for regression towards her old suicidal behaviors. I advised her about the rationale for this and reassured her that my precautions were in no way meant to be punitive.

The next day, Angela appeared to be a little better. We talked about how we could move on from this and how to learn from what had happened. Angela expressed her despondency, as it seemed to her that her own mother did not love her since she had sided with the man who raped her. I explained to her that we could not control her mother's actions, statements or behaviors, but we can learn to control our own actions. I told her that I was so proud of her progress that day, and that we could build on today's progress. In order to do so, I had Angela make a list of everything that she was grateful for in her life. I told her it could be anything. I taught her **Principle Seven**: **Have an attitude of gratitude.** I asked Angela to come up with a list of ten positive things per day. I explained to Angela that since whatever she focused on she would feel, our focus would be upon the positive things in her life. As Angela began to focus on the positive, everything changed. Angela climbed up the unit's reward level system and went to the top in about a week.

She was feeling so well afterwards that she wanted to go on a pass with her father, Ken. Angela's father appeared to be very supportive and was coming to all of the family sessions that we had scheduled with him. I told her father that she could have up to ten hours on a pass. I also explained to her father that he needed to watch her, and if he felt that she needed to come back earlier, bring her back. We agreed on a ten-hour pass. Ken picked her up at 11a.m. and told us that they would be back at 9p.m.

I had this particular weekend off. When I arrived on Monday for work, I discovered that Angela had not come back until Sunday at 9pm. Since this was twenty-four hours late, I inquired as to what took place. It seemed that because her father had to go to work, he let Angela stay with a friend of the family. Since Ken knew the friend since his childhood, Ken told him about what had been taking place with the daughter.

Then a bombshell dropped. Tragedy struck again. Angela told me that the family friend had molested her and told her not to tell anyone. The family friend said that he had been attracted to her for quite some time. Further, (like most sex abusers do) he warned her that if she told her father what had happened, it would ruin not only the friendship between the two men, but it would also end the friendship that Angela already had with the man's daughter. Angela explained, "Since I'm very good friends with his daughter, I don't want to tell my father what took place."

Angela told me that Paul, the family friend, gave her some wine, telling her it would be their secret. I told Angela that she needed to take some responsibility for drinking at age fourteen, but I also explained to her that what had happened to her was not her fault. I let her know that we would need to work on her issues, help her with her history of being molested, teach her about boundary issues and that we would need to tell her father what had happened.

When we had our family session with the father, we explained to him what had happened. Ken became despondent, wondering aloud how a lifelong friend could hurt him by molesting his daughter. Ken appeared very pained and in stark contrast to Angela's mother; Ken believed his daughter. He explained to Angela that this should have never taken place, regretting not returning to the hospital on time and telling Paul about Angela's recent sexual assaults. Furthermore, he became so upset that he said he was going to kill Paul for doing this—which surprised both Angela and me.

As we processed what took place together, I reminded Ken of the consequences of killing Paul. (Of course, I realize that many people say things they do not mean when they are under extreme stress). I told him that I would be filing an abuse report and to please let the legal system handle it. Upon agreeing to this, Ken asked me how he could become a better father and relate to his daughter. I told him about the seven principles that I use all the time in my work with teens and their parents. I also gave him examples of how to use them in his own life.

In review, these seven principles are:

- **Teach something of value to your teen, and then help them to have a reason or purpose.**
- **Find one thing to do with your teen.**
- **Parents should do something for their teen, but nothing material.**
- **Give your child something of yours.**
- **Ask your teen for conversation.**
- **Tell your child you love them.**
- **Have an attitude of gratitude.**

I explained to Ken that he needed to practice the seven principles on a daily basis. I reassured him that he was a great father, but Angela was in need of much support. They needed to have family time at least once a week to talk about everything and build an even stronger bond.

After the family session, I continued to work with Angela in individual sessions, where we worked on her self-esteem, trust, boundary challenges and the way she perceives men. We identified ways for Angela to work on her sexual assault issues and I encouraged her to seek ongoing help. Angela worked very hard to achieve the outcome that she wanted, completing all of my assignments. Despite what had happened to her, when she went home, Angela had a different perspective on life. She understood that what had taken place was now in her past, that she could handle any triggers and defuse them, and finally, that the past does not equal the future.

Angela also learned that the choices she makes today *can* change her destiny forever. I explained to Angela that everything that happens (even bad things) could be viewed as happening for a reason or a purpose to serve her. This means that every event that takes place *can* make you stronger. Since she could learn from this, Angela could make sure that she did not repeat these same situations over again. I showed Angela how to reframe things so as to ask better questions, how to listen to her gut feelings more and how to continue with a daily 'attitude of gratitude' list.

Angela left the hospital with a big smile and thanked me for everything. When she whispered in my ear that she wanted to be a singer, I smiled and asked her to sing for me. She sang *"I wish upon a star"* and I understood why she was named Angela, as she has a voice like an angel. I hoped that she would pursue her goal. Last I heard, Angela was working on her challenges and doing great, and her father practices the seven principles on a daily basis.

### Letter from Angela after leaving the hospital

John, John, John, Well hmmm . . .

I'm going to miss you so much. At first I was pretty mean to you, but you also picked on me too, but it did me some good. It made me stronger. You worked to build my self-esteem, like write 30 positive a day. I know that it was to help me and it DID!

Thank you! You gave me words of wisdom. I'll keep them and use them! You were the most wonderful therapist ever! I'll always remember you as TALL! [You are also] compassionate, wise, strong, and a very sincere person!

### THANK YOU FOR ALL YOUR HELP!

Angela

> P.S. Thanks for making me do this, because secretly I always wanted to be a singer (our little secret, okay?)

### Case Five

I was asked by the State of Oregon to take this next case. '"Robert" has been in and out of treatment and his behavior has not been anything to brag about. When I met his mother, she appeared very frightened by his violent outbursts and did not want to take care of him. All his life, his father had often told Robert that since he is superior to women, they needed to bow down to him. Robert's father had immigrated here from another country, and was not an American citizen. Robert's father taught him the **first principle** but in a negative way. He taught him a value, and then he reinforced it with reason or purpose—but the value Robert's dad taught him was negative because it would not help Robert in the real world of modern America. It further led to difficulties for Robert because it was insensitive and biased against women.

Robert had seen his father treat his mother in a rude and disrespectful way as a child and continued to see him demean her as a teen. His mother submitted to this abuse, so in his mindset, he thought this behavior was the way females should be treated. When Robert was about six years old, his father went to the store and never came back. When his father left, Robert's behavior changed and his mother had a living nightmare on her hands. Robert became like his father. He would treat his mother like a dog, hit her, cuss at her, and generally make her feel terrible.

Robert's mother, Wendy, could not talk to Robert at all, nor could she get him to listen. Although Wendy took Robert to counseling, she discovered many counselors did not want to work with him due to his rude, explosive behavior and his belittling of females. If the therapist were a woman, he would treat her with severe disrespect. Most of his therapists stated that Robert would never change his behavior because he had learned these dysfunctional rules so early in life, asserting that he would never get better. This diagnosis would make discourage any patient and cause him to give up or think, 'What's the use in trying?' By communicating this to him, and by Robert's acceptance of these beliefs, these therapists had unwittingly created a self-fulfilling prophecy, something that educational psychologists call the Pygmalion, or Rosenthal Effect.

Since Robert was so difficult to manage, his mother moved him in with relatives. She decided she could not longer cope with his temper, rage and disrespectful attitude. She was unaware of the fact that she would sometimes inadvertently trigger his behaviors by her actions. Robert's stay with his aunt and uncle was a nightmare to say the least. His aunt was very demanding and pushy and his uncle appeared to be his friend until the wife came home, and then he pushed young Robert around like a rag doll. Again, Robert received mixed signals.

When I came into the picture, it was his first week at his aunt and uncle's house. In our work, I defined a system of levels for him. That is, I gave him goals to work on and rewards along the way. I gave him a level system because I knew he needed structure in the household. I felt like young Robert never had any structure. I explained to Robert about the importance of being respectful towards his family. At the same time, I knew why this was a challenge. The behavior of his aunt and uncle would not induce respect in anyone. He would have to respect them in principle, while learning tools in our work together that would help him modify his negative behaviors.

He would have to be taught to respect the integrity of his family, while finding the strength to work on his goals without the family's interest. Sometimes teens have to be taught to work on their issues and goals outside of the home because their home life is not yet able to provide the structure needed for this to happen. Still, the teen has to cope with that home life. That is, he or she must want to change and by his or her actual change, may actually cause positive changes to the entire family.

Robert agreed to work with me and to follow my rules, as I had explained to him that I would call all the shots. Robert needed this since changing his negative behaviors required a great amount work and there was some urgency to the issue as we would only be working together for a short period of time (meaning less than a year).

When Robert explained to me that all his previous therapists told him he would never get better, I told Robert that was their belief, that we all have different beliefs about life and that therapists might even have differing beliefs about clients. I stressed to him that it is up to him, not the other therapists, to believe whatever he wants to about himself, but those beliefs, positive or negative, can be very powerful. Secondly, I educated him through story telling about people who face challenge in their lives and how they change through hard work. Such beliefs can change what people say about themselves and outwardly, their behaviors. Further, I emphasized to him that changing his behaviors would even change how others viewed him. Finally, I stressed to him that we would be focusing on the positive beliefs that would make it all happen for him. I also explained to Robert that all his life he had simply been reactive and my goal would be to make him proactive. Being proactive would help him to control his behaviors and change how other people viewed him. When I asked him if he was ready to get to work, it turned out that Robert was eager to get things done.

Since we had now established a working agreement, I told Robert what I expected of him. First of all, he would need to go to groups every week. These groups would center on my other teen-focused treatment philosophies such as: **The 7 Principles of Highly Self-Motivated Teens**, and later on, **Bonding the Family Together.**

Not only would he be in groups with people his own age, he would also be required to attend both individual and family sessions biweekly. When Robert asked me if this would make him better, I told him (as I do always-- to instill a sense of expectancy) that these programs would change his life. I told Robert we had a journey to complete together, and with the right attitude, we could turn things around.

Week one in the group we worked on breaking through fears and limitations. We had a 'board break' (a simple karate technique described earlier) that represents life challenges. First, we drew an X in the middle of the board and listed everything we must break through in our lives on the back of the board. We also wrote down what we wanted these things to change into (desired outcomes). One example of what Robert wrote down was poor school grades and he wanted to 'break through it by earning B's on his report card.

First, I gave Robert instructions that all of his focus should be on the desired outcomes, not the negative things themselves that he wanted to change. By doing so, the act of breaking the board would become a metaphor for each student that would represent the complete process of the negative and the catalyst for achieving the positive. Each could then say, "I have done it! The past is behind me, and I'll reach my goals!"

When all of the students broke their boards, it was perceived and anchored as a major event. In one moment, they believed they had stopped their previous patterns of behavior and were ready to move onto their targeted accomplishments. I feel this is a great metaphor that people should adopt in their lives. If everyone focused on what they wanted, or must have in their lives, rather than what they did not want, they would obtain their goals. Robert seemed very happy to break the board, especially because beforehand he did not believe that he would be able to break a real board. I told him he needed to face his challenges in life the very same way. I told Robert to focus on the outcomes, and not on the way he wants to feel, what he might see or his circumstances. Robert needed to learn to change his state and even those negative feelings that hinder him. I encouraged Robert to rise about the negativity and change his mindset by adopting new beliefs about possibility.

He went home to his aunt and uncle's house in such a magnificent mood, willing to take on any challenge. When he got home he already had to use the tools he learned in class. His aunt seemed to be in a nasty mood since she cooked some food for Robert and Robert did not want to eat that food. Robert asked her if he could have a sandwich instead. The aunt angrily told him no. She also told him if he did not eat the food she had cooked, he would not be allowed to eat anything.

He thought about it for a couple of minutes and told her he would eat it. The aunt said it was too late and took away the food. Of course, this upset Robert very much. Robert remembered what he had learned in group that day about not looking at his circumstances but instead to look at what he must feel, so Robert thought about being happy, and not letting her steal his joy from him. So Robert walked away from that potential confrontation and went in his bedroom to listen to music. His aunt followed him and began yelling and screaming at him, telling him that he should be happy to be in a nice house like this. Robert gave me a call at my office so I could listen to what was happening at home. I overheard his aunt telling his uncle how Robert was being disrespectful to her and that he should take care of it now.

When his uncle came into the room, I heard him yelling that Robert should never treat his wife like that after she had cooked for him. He also threatened Robert, stating, "I should kick your ass!" This was followed by a dial tone. After about ten minutes, the uncle called me, telling me about Robert threatening to kill him, so he hit him several times. I asked him what started the entire thing and I noted that the uncle lied to me about what had happened and blamed Robert for everything. The uncle did not know it was I who had been on the phone.

I had to report what I heard regarding poor treatment and physical abuse by the uncle to the State. The next week, we had a family session. Robert's mother, uncle, aunt and his little sister all attended. I wanted to find out what was happening in the household, and then, to find ways to work out the issues. I confronted the uncle and aunt on their abusive behaviors and told them they needed to find a way to be connected with Robert, not make him fear them. They asked me how I could believe anything that Robert said because of his past. I explained to them that Robert's past did not equal his future. I further went on that people can change, including Robert, and that there are two sides to every story and everyone should be heard. I described my techniques and how they could connect with Robert through use of **The 7 Principles of Connecting with Your Teen**. All three of the adults stated, "I don't need that. I raised three grown children. It's not us, it's Robert."

I told them that something was wrong with their picture of things, that they needed to alter their belief system and that I could readily see why it was hard for Robert to take responsibility for his actions. Basically, they were repeatedly modeling some of the very same negative behaviors from within the family. Consequently, a number of his 'problematic' behaviors were learned behaviors. I could already see that he learned many of his actions and beliefs from his relatives. Robert talked to his mother about how she treated his sister like a queen, but gave him little respect. Robert's mother, Wendy, responded by stating that his sister is nice and is her best friend. When Wendy stated: "I tell your sister everything," I asked Wendy if she thought it was wise to confide in her eight-year-old daughter like she would an adult. Wendy ignored me and continued making excuses. Wendy went on to say, "Robert looks like his father, so every time I see Robert he reminds me of his father."

Robert had previously told his group of peers that his mother had told him that he was going to be like his father, that he would never get better, he would have a low IQ and he would never become anything in his life. I then asked his mother if she had made those statements. When Wendy replied that she had, she retorted that it was only for his own good so that he would know how his life would be and could prepare for it. This was flawed, fatalistic thinking. If Robert bought into these negative prophecies, I knew that is how is life would be. At that point, I was confident that with the right coaching, he would overcome all those years of negative expectancies he had taken in. I knew when Wendy concluded her speech with "there's nothing left for me to do, but to pray for him," that Robert and I would have to work together without his family's help or support; but in that working together, we would be able to do it. Of course, in doing so, I also hoped that some of this work would rub off on Robert's family, too.

The next session with Robert was an individual session. We talked about his prior family session, what had taken place and how we can build off all the exciting information and different belief systems Robert had. (Sounds like a sell job, just short of a placebo—but I am not one to rob a hurting individual of hope!) I said that everyone might have his or her own opinion about everything and that it is just an opinion. I emphasized to him that we make our own destiny, and if we uncritically believe what other people say about us, then we will prove them right. I told Robert my goal would be to empower him in a positive way so that he could control his own destiny.

Robert went through the entire seven weeks of group and made great efforts to change his mindset. Living at his aunt and uncle's house was not getting better at all, as the yelling continue and worsened, and they would even put Robert out of the house on cold days because they did not want to bother with him. It seemed like they would antagonize him, just to see him get angry and try to sabotage things so that nothing would work. A struggling boy had made a radical change and the environmental pressures tried to pull him right back down. I knew Robert was hungry to change and that was one of the best things he had going for him. It was a beginning place—a place that would catapult him to transcendence of those environmental stressors.

One day he seemed to have hit his threshold. He came home from school in a pretty good mood and wanted to have a snack. His aunt and uncle told him no, so Robert explained to them, even showing them on a contract they had written out together, that this should be snack time. His aunt replied harshly, "This is our food, not yours!"

His uncle also continued to be nice to Robert when the aunt was not present, and predictably, when his wife would get home the uncle would change his attitude. On this day, his uncle was extremely angry because he had just applied for a job and did not get it (in psychology, we call this displacement). So he vented his anger on Robert. On top of that, the aunt always seemed to be in a nasty mood around Robert, and that day it was severe. The uncle joked with Robert about Robert's mother having a 'stupid' job, with to which

Robert responded that at least she had a job.  Once again, he struck Robert several times and then his aunt kicked him outside.  Robert called me at my office telling me what took place.  I came out to the house and the aunt told me a different story. She stated that Robert had pulled a knife on the uncle and that was why the uncle hit him.  I told everyone to call the police because I wanted to get Robert out of that house.  The police came to the house and sent Robert to the hospital.

Looking back at this situation the aunt and uncle never connected with young Robert. Here are some questions to help us analyze the situation:

1)  *Did they teach Robert something of value, and then the purpose and reason why?*

Not at all. They believed that they had all the answers.  They only taught him negative actions and behaviors, such as lying cheating and stealing.

2)  *Did they find one thing to do with their teen?*

No, they did not include young Robert into any activities.

3)  *Did they do something with their teen.?*

Absolutely nothing.

4)  *Did they give something to their teen?*

Maybe to their own three grown children…but not to Robert.

5)  *Did they ask for conversation?*

Not in a positive way.  They yelled, screamed and called Robert names.

6)  *Did they tell him they loved him?*

Never.

7)  *Did they have an attitude of gratitude?*

Not at all.

Can you see why they never connected with Robert? Can you understand the difference it would have made? Can you understand the importance of using these seven principles in your family life?

Back to the case, Robert was at the hospital for about eight days. At the hospital, he did not learn anything other than that he was in a holding cell. The hospital taught him how to be thankful for what he did have at his aunt and uncle's house since the stay was that unpleasant and no progress took place. Still, I knew that no one should be subject to any type of abuse, so Robert could not go back to the aunt and uncle's house and he would have to find somewhere else to stay. Anyone can become a biological parent—but I feel so many do not know how to really parent. I wish people were all mandated to attend classes on parenting. Many of life's challenges with our youth would not happen if that were the case. So, after the brief stay in the hospital, we sent Robert to live in a residential home. We told him he needed to stay for about two months. Robert was informed that he would not be returning to his aunt and uncle's house.

Robert went to the residential house and seemed to have a difficult time making friends. The staff told me that he would never get past Level Two, but I told the staff that Robert would be on the top level before the eight weeks were finished. They responded that it is nice to be positive, but after reading Robert's chart seeing him at the house for the past ten days, they could not see it happening. I let them know that although I respected their opinions, they should never tell Robert what they were thinking. (I also wanted to shock them out of unconsciously communicating hopelessness to Robert in any way, since this is what he had already seen in his young life). So, I admonished them to not create Robert's belief system like his relatives had already done throughout all of his life. If anything, it told me anew that the power of negative labels transcends families and can even be a part of a system that is trying to help someone.

Since I wanted Robert to see the possibility of changing the quality of his life through changing his belief system, I kept reminding him what I expected from him. For the first two weeks, Robert remained on the entry level with no progress made in the treatment center's structure. I decided to have one-on-one sessions with Robert to help him change his mindset and to empower him. During our first session, we talked about the influence his father had on his life. I had him look at his negative expectations and helped him reframe them by looking at positive counter beliefs. We also worked on his abandonment issues about his father leaving him and his family. I showed him how to release all the pain by taking it and turning it into pleasure so it can help him instead of hurt him. After the session, Robert told me that he felt light, like he had removed all the pain from his life.

Robert returned to the treatment house in a different mindset, almost like a changed person after only one session. I did not see Robert for about ten days, but when I returned Robert had progressed up to level two. The entire staff appeared to be shocked, and for the first time in his life, Robert received praise and everyone was talking about his positive changes. We had another one-on-one, and this time we played his favorite sport, basketball. I wanted to see his anger, and since I was a former college player, I beat him badly, and predictably, he did become angry. After I witnessed his anger on the basketball court, I knew how I would treat him in our future individual sessions. We would work on his anger, where I would show him how to use his anger as an ally, so it could support his outcome. We would use different techniques until I felt something worked for him.

After another ten days passed by, (it would have been about twenty-one days total) Robert was on the highest level. The staff told me that nobody in treatment there had been able to reach that level for two years and the longest that someone had stayed on level four was one week. I told the staff that Robert would be on this level until he left treatment. They looked at me like I was crazy; however, Robert did leave on the highest level, working daily on producing changes in his life. He followed the seven weeks' group schedule and he applied what he learned from groups in his own life. He found out how he could break through his fear and limitations with his family, he made a mission statement and he had carefully designed goals. He also found out how to communicate with other people without showing disrespect. Basically, he was learning how to function as a responsible human being!

After this, Robert wanted to work on a relationship with his mother because they had never understood one another. I told Robert I had a new program and I wanted him and his mother to attend it. It was called "**Bonding the Family Together**." The program required three days of participation, with my goals being to transform families and build trust, love, and respect among the family members. We had ten families in my first seminar. I wanted all of the families to participate in group activities and learn how they functioned as a unit. The first thing we worked on was communication between family members. I had the parents work together in one group and the teens in another group. The desired outcome was to show both sides how to communicate in a positive way and to learn how to respect each other.

As "Bonding the Family Together" progressed, we went through communication skills, forgiving the family, the pain of not changing and pleasure for changing. At one point, Robert confronted his mother about her behavior in a positive way. I felt he needed to let some steam out. This could possibly be a breakthrough for him (potentially for both of them). Later, I recalled that he had told me he had never told his mother how he had felt in his entire lifetime. Wendy did not say anything when Robert confronted her. She blamed everything on his father and told the group that she would be praying for him. Robert told his mother that she always hides behind her religion and never deals with anything. Robert was very assertive using "I" statements instead of blaming "you" statements, and again his mother appeared to be avoiding him in her answers. Robert told his mother the way he felt about everything and told her that she needed to be a mother. He also added that she should not try to be his friend. Tears came to his eyes and rolled down his cheeks when he insisted he did not want to talk to her until she could be honest with him.

When this happened, the other parents in the room rallied themselves to Robert's cause, and for the first time, Robert knew what it meant to have support. He felt the strength from the entire group backing him up. Wendy played the victim role and the other parents in the room told her that her child needed a response to his concerns. Wendy had to answer difficult questions for the first time in her life. Robert said: "I hate you for telling me that I would be like my father, I hate you for treating my sister better than me and I hate you for telling me that I had a learning disability! Why did you do this?" Wendy told the group her reasons for telling her son this information, but her rationale fell apart. That day would surely represent a turning point for both Robert and his mom.

One of the other parents stated, "You should love your children, and I feel your son came out just great because even though he never had any role models to look up to, he's doing just great!" Wendy wept even more and began to make excuses and Robert said to her "I wish you would tell the truth for the first time in your life." Wendy told Robert that he looked just like her ex-husband, and every time she saw Robert it reminded her of his Dad and then she felt all the abuse her ex had put the family through.

Robert boldly challenged her to choose not to see him this way, in other words, to choose to not let him function as a trigger for recall of her past traumas. Then he verbally admonished his mom with loving comments about how it was "time to move on, and to focus on the present not the past." Wendy was visibly moved.

Robert now had all the support from the group, and they responded in kind, with other mothers in the group confronting Wendy on her behaviors and explaining to her that she needed to use the **seven principles** to connect with her teen:

- **Teach Robert something of value, and the reason and purpose.**
- **Find something to do with Robert.**
- **Do something for Robert, nothing material.**
- **Give Robert something of yours.**
- **Ask Robert for conversation.**
- **Tell Robert that you love him.**
- **Have an attitude of gratitude towards him.**

One of the parents in the group stated that not only should Wendy use the seven principles with Robert, but also with her daughter. Another mother reinforced this idea, by saying that Wendy should treat all of her children the same in order for them to bond together. After group, Robert did not want to go home with his mother because he was very angry with her. I told Robert he would not be able to stay with me, but he needed to love his mother and have some healing time with her. I also told him that we were now ready to have our final session tomorrow. Wendy rejoined Robert and I at this point, and after I told them good night, we agreed to meet each other at 11 a.m. the next morning.

On the last day of the seminar most of the families seemed to bond together. Robert and his mother came on the last day with big smiles on their faces. Still, during the session, Wendy told the group that she resented my having the group confront her, and she felt that was not fair—but in her next breath she revealed that the confrontation had worked!  Wendy announced that she and Robert had really talked for the first time and worked on their challenges. Wendy told the group that she would adopt the seven principles in her life and that she wanted a relationship with her son.

Since "**Bonding the Family Together,**" Robert and his mother have been getting along.  This was the first time ever that Robert would spend an entire harmonious weekend at his mother's house.  Now, Robert wants to stay permanently with his mother and have a real family.  Robert is in high school and is getting *A's* and *B's* and says he wants to be a military man and have a family of his own.  His attitudes changed in so many ways that he has been a positive influence on others.  He communicates well with people and treats all women much better.  He comes to coaching sessions with me every quarter to work on small challenges.  He is one of the most successful cases the State has ever seen, because this process took only four months.  I always told Robert change happens in a moment, but Robert has proven something that I have seen over and over in my career: *people can change if they will only believe it.*

You see, I have shared these Case Summaries for a reason—that they may provide hope and inspiration to you.  I hope they have challenged you!

My sincerest hope for you, dear readers, is that you will find a way to use my principles to help you with your teens.  I also pray that you will be helped to find the power to institute self-directed change by changing your beliefs into positive ones!  Happy parenting and happy living!  Thanks for reading my book!

Dr. John Oda

## *A Letter from a Parent*

Dear Dr. Oda:

The purpose of this letter is to inform you about the outcome of your program—The Seven Techniques of Highly Self-Motivated Teens. My daughter feels that her participation in this program has allowed her to learn more about herself and how to achieve her goals more effectively. I have to admit that her beliefs are more definitely on target. Your class has helped my daughter pursue her goals in a more effective way. I feel that she always knew what she wanted, but teenagers tend to listen to other people better than parents. I am glad that the person was YOU, because you are a highly motivated individual with a lot of teenage outlook in your persona.

Please provide me with information about your session to come, because we would like to participate again.

Sincerely,

*Marcela, Beaverton Parent*

# Special Addenda: Excerpts from Dr. Oda's Columns

## "THE DOCTOR'S CORNER"

Dear Dr. John:

I'm a seventeen-year-old white male and I'm going out with a black female the same age. My parents don't approve of this girl because she's black. I really like her a lot, and I want my parents to see past her color. What should I do?

*Torn Apart*

Dear Torn Apart,

Thanks for writing. I can understand you're feeling torn. I feel you need to talk with your parents, telling them how you feel about this person. If that doesn't work, speak with a pastor or a professional in the mental health field. I would also look into what's shaping your parent's belief system and why they're opposed to the relationship.

Something that might be helpful to you, your girlfriend and your parents would be to make a list of pros and cons in an effort to see how this situation might be worked out. At seventeen, sometimes things can seem larger than they are. If you really care for this girl, you can wait until you move out of the house to pursue the relationship.

If your parents don't want you to see this girl, it's best to follow their wishes. It would also be best to seek counseling so that you and your parents won't be torn apart.

Make your life outstanding!

Dr. John Oda

Dear Dr. John:

I'm a senior in high school, and I've been accepted to a private college out of state on a full scholarship. I just found out that I'm pregnant. I have been thinking about getting an abortion. I come from a Christian family and I have been taught that abortion is wrong. I'm wondering: Should I put off going to college, or should I have an abortion? HELP!

Dear Help:

Thanks for writing. I want to congratulate you for getting a full ride. The first thing you must do is take responsibility for your actions. Then begin to explore your options. Here are a few good, simple ways to get started:

- Find someone your age who has had a baby and who is still pursuing her dreams of going to college.
- Do some research on abortion.
- Do some research on adoption.

People say that knowledge is power, but I disagree. Rather, I believe that knowledge is *potential* power. ACTION is power!

Now take some action and talk with your parents, explaining to them how you feel. If you can't speak to your parents, connect with your pastor, school counselor or a professional in the mental health field. Once you obtain the knowledge and begin to take some action steps, you'll find your answer.

Make your fate!

Dr. John Oda

Dear Dr. John:

I'm worried about my eighteen-year-old son who's a senior in high school. He has a 4.0 GPA and hasn't applied to any colleges, even though everyone has been pressuring him to get started. My son told me that college is not the place for him. What should I do?

*Concerned*

Dear Concerned:

Thanks for writing. It appears that you want the best for your son. So it's time to support your son's decision. As you said, he is eighteen, and appears that he's calling the shots. Great!

Now find out how he plans to support himself when he graduates from high school. He can't think he'll still be living at home for free, right? He has to get his own apartment, transportation, buy his food and much, much, more. Since our economy is so unpredictable now and so many people are out of work, he may not find a job. Let's say he does find a job and earns $7.00 per hour. At forty hours per week that's about $280.00 per week, or $1120.00 per month. After taxes, he'll have something like $840.00 per month.

Let's see how he can make it:

Rent $400-$550 (plus a first and last, and possible security deposits)
Food $100
Car Insurance $200
Car Payment $150-$250

First of all, can he survive on $100 worth of groceries each month? What if he gets sick? He very possibly won't have health insurance, so maybe his monthly income might even be less. Perhaps he could join the military or reconsider going to college. Since I feel everyone should have a choice, I hope your son recognizes he has many choices. I also hope that he thoughtfully considers them all while there's time. Eventually, his choices will be fewer.

Make your life outstanding!

Dr John Oda

Dear Dr. John:

I'm fifteen and I want to have my nose pierced and my parents told me that I could not. I feel like it's my body and it shouldn't make any difference to them. They shouldn't tell me what to do. What should I do?

*Angry in Portland*

Dear Angry in Portland,

Thanks for writing. It seems that you want to have your cake and eat it too. Sometimes life seems unfair and we want to do something with which our loved ones disagree. Your stance as you described it seems selfish to me. Did you do any research on getting your nose pierced? Do you know about side effects? Here are a few:

- You can get an infection in your nose.
- You will have a permanent scar on your face.
- If seeking a job, most employers won't take you seriously. You'll lose the job at the interview.

You need to listen to your parents and obey their rules. Sometimes you might feel they're being hard on you, but usually, they're interested in helping you. Perhaps you can explore other ways to express your uniqueness?

When you turn eighteen and move out on your own, you can make your own rules. Until then, listen to your parents!

Make your fate!

Dr. John Oda

Dear Dr. John:

I'm sixteen and lately life hasn't been treating me well, despite the fact that my family is well off and we live in a very nice neighborhood. My problem is that I get very depressed over the littlest things. I'm not that popular in school. Some people have told me that I'm very "passive," and I'm pretty much a loner. Sometimes I think about suicide because I really feel that people don't like me.

I've dropped hints to my parents, but I'm scared to death of telling them. Even if I DARE to write something sad, they dismiss it as "morbid" and refuse to read it. What should I do?

*Angel*

Dear Angel:

Thanks for writing. This sounds like a tough time for you and it also sound like you are very confused. A good first step would be to talk to your parents—tell them what's going on. If you still feel you can't reach them, tell your counselor at school or your pastor at church. You might find these folks helpful, or you might even have them help you with family counseling with is very much available.

Another possibility is to go online and visit The American Association of Suicidology at www.suicidology.org. The site has an online directory for suicide crisis centers and a directory for local hotlines. One such hotline, run by the National Hope Line Network, is 1-800-SUICIDE (800-784-2433). It's available twenty-four hours a day. Please call it immediately and tell them exactly what are you experiencing.

Remember: confusion presents an opportunity to learn about yourself and find new ways for dealing with challenges in life. Such challenges can seem really big at sixteen years old.

Angel, you are loved by your parents, friends, teachers and many others. Trust that and the truth that you are NOT alone. Reach out for the help that's out there and anxious to hear from YOU!

See you on the top!

Dr. John Oda

Dear Dr. John:

I'm a high school senior and I have been going with my boyfriend for three months. My boyfriend is pressuring me to have sex. I love him a lot and don't want to lose him. What should I do?

*Confused in Portland*

Dear Confused:

Thanks for writing. I feel you should only have sex when you are mentally and physically ready. It appears that you are not and having second thoughts. Always trust your gut.

If your boyfriend truly loved you, he would never pressure you into having sex. In life, there are always consequences. Let's examine some that relate specifically to having sex. Starting with one of the biggies, are you ready to be a mother, to commit the next eighteen years of your life to raising a child? Would your boyfriend join you, or would he leave?

The next biggie, of course, is STDs (sexually transmitted diseases). Remember, if you sleep with someone, you have slept with everyone they have. How's your self-esteem? Do you really love yourself? If you're not sure, a little work in that area could do wonders.

When in doubt, a simple yet powerful tool is to consider life's consequences before taking action. Ask yourself, "What is this going to cost me a year from now?" I hope you make the right decision. Speak with your parents or school counselor.

Make Your Fate!

Dr John Oda

Dear Dr. John:

I am a senior in high school. My parents have been pressuring me about my grades. My G.P.A. is 3.6 and I play basketball, football and track. I'm very active in school. My parents feel that I should be getting a 4.0. Their demands make me feel stressed and depressed. I feel like I'm always trying to please them. People in my school think I have the perfect life because I'm always smiling. In reality, I have very low self-esteem. How can I work things out with my parents?

HELP!

Dear Help:

Thank you for writing. You appear to be doing an outstanding job—pat yourself on the back! Anyone making outstanding grades, playing sports and engaging in school activities all at the same time is doing a great job in my book.

I feel that you and your parents would benefit from counseling geared to clarify their rules. Good for you for recognizing that you need to work on yourself. It's time to take off your mask and deal with your challenges. If you're always smiling, there's a good chance you're putting on a mask, at least some of the time. Work on yourself and find a counselor you can relate to. Keep up the outstanding job!

See ya on the top!

Dr. John Oda

Dear Dr. John:

I am an eighteen-year-old woman attending college fulltime. I also dance three hours every day. Also, I work part-time 8 hours every Friday, Saturday, and Sunday. Plus, I have a boyfriend. I don't have any time to myself, but I don't want to cut out any of my current activities. What should I do?

*Tired in NE Portland*

Dear Tired:

Many people your age face similar challenges. It's time to check your priorities and consider a new plan for your day. Let's have some fun creating a life that you can enjoy and not be so worn-out. Put things in proper perspective and your life won't seem so overwhelming.

Start with a system. First, you've got to do the important thing first, and then the others. A plan that might help is my G-5 system that considers each activity, or segment of your life and puts it in order of priority. For example:

G-5 is the most important thing that must get done first. For example, going to class and your dancing.

G-4 is working on the weekend.

G-3 is having time with your boyfriend.

G-2 is hanging out with your friends.

G-1 is playing computer games.

If you need to pick yourself up a planner, do it so that you can write down important dates, events and school assignments. I also feel a planner will free up more time for you and your activities. If you take about twenty minutes each week to plan your big events, appointments or assignments from school this will free up a lot of time. I also suggest that you use the G-5 system to determine what's most important and what activities should become your 'first thing first'.

It's best to have **four** "rocks" that you do on a weekly basis. For example, the **first** rock might be to go to dance class. The **second** rock is study for a math quiz, the **third** rock, work on a term paper that's due next week and the **fourth** rock is time to spend with your boyfriend.

It's good idea to write down a brief summary of *why* you want to accomplish these rocks, because as human beings we tend to focus on two simple things: pain and pleasure. In fact, we will do almost anything to gain pleasure, and likewise, almost anything to avoid pain. You are now experiencing the pain of not having your rocks in order.

By making a schedule, you'll actually build in free time as a part of it, which with so much going on all the time – might just be the only way you'll really make that happen.

Enjoy your years!

Dr. John Oda

Dear Dr. John:

I think my boyfriend of two years might be cheating on me with my best friend. I am not sure how to deal with this. I need help.

*Confused in Chicago*

Dear Confused:

Thanks for writing. Surely you're feeling confused by what's taking place. I suggest that you first find out if what you're feeling is a result of your own insecurities or events that are really taking place. If you're a little insecure, it's best to work on your self-esteem, and find new ways to love yourself.

If it turns out that he is cheating on you, it's best to confront the challenge directly and in an assertive way. Two good techniques to consider in addressing such a situation are to use "I" statements and to say how you feel in a positive way.

For example, "I feel __ when you do _____." And, yes you should give him an example. I would also suggest you speak with your best friend and explain to her how you're feeling as well. Remember to be assertive. Now keep in mind that to be assertive is not to be aggressive, passive aggressive or passive. It means being respectful and direct, appropriate and honest. Use "I" statements and explain to them how you feel. Finally, if you find that he's cheating, at your age, it's best to break up and move on.

See ya at the top!

Dr. John Oda

Dear Dr. John:

My dog died about two months ago. We had him for several years and I'm having nightmares about it. I really miss him! How can I get over my sadness caused by this absence and my upset feelings over his death?

*Distraught in NE, Portland*

Dear Distraught:

Thanks for writing. You're going through a tough time right now. The loss of a pet is very much like the loss of a family member, and your grief should be treated accordingly. I suggest that you find a way to say goodbye to your dog. This can be done in the form of a letter, talking about your pet and your feelings with a trusted friend or even by holding a ceremony of some kind.

If the dog is buried near your home for example, you might create a loving marker. If not, you might still place or plant flowers in a special spot in the yard to commemorate him. Another helpful activity can be writing your feelings and thoughts in a journal. Sometimes putting things on paper can help you sort through your feelings and find a sense of closure.

Another activity that sometimes works well for the grieving is considering your attitude and finding reasons for gratitude. By writing down the things you're thankful you experienced because of your pet, you might be able to shift your focus from feeling anger that he's gone to feeling truly glad for the time he was there—a much better space.

Finally, I would suggest that you talk it over with your family because they're probably going through the same challenges. Grieving the loss of a loved one—yes even a pet, takes time. Be gentle with yourself and let time heal you. It will.

Dr. John Oda

Dear Dr. John:

I'm a sixteen-year-old male. I have been teased all my life about being fat. I'm 5'11 and weigh 270 pounds. I don't have a girlfriend and I don't have many friends. Every year I have been making the same New Year's resolution to lose weight and I haven't been able to stick to it. I would like to weigh 210 pounds. What should I do?

*Discouraged in Indiana*

Dear Discouraged:

Thanks for writing. A lot of people make New Year's resolutions and very few really do follow through on them to achieve them. So, first know you're not alone. Second, anytime is a good time to take some action. Like now! Briefly, I'd like you to consider a system called O.P.A.

First thing, you must establish your **desired outcome.** For example, you want to weigh 210 pounds, have a 33-inch waist and the 12% body fat. That's your desired outcome.

Next, determine your **purpose**—Why do you want to lose weight? Write down fifty reasons.

Third, you need a **plan**—What do you have to do to get the weight off? A new way of eating? An exercise program? Maybe it would help to write down everything you eat.

Finally, the system only works when you do it. **Take action today**. Read up on different ways to lose weight. Now is also a great time to visualize how you want to look. Do this in the morning and night. I would suggest that you also put some effort into your self-esteem. A helpful exercise is to say three positive statements about yourself out loud daily. And write them down. It also sometimes helps to model your approach after someone you know who has lost weight and kept it off. Keep in touch. I'll see you on the top!

Dr. John Oda

Dear Dr. John:

I have a fourteen-year-old daughter who wants to be a model. We went to a modeling school where they told us that she has "the look." My daughter became very excited, as she wants to be a professional model. The salesperson told her that there was only one spot open and advised her to take it right away. He told us that the program would improve her self-esteem and her grades. I, too, wanted her to become a model until the salesperson told us about the hidden costs. He wanted us to pay $1500.00! As a concerned mother, is it worth paying that much?

*Worried in Vancouver*

Dear Worried:

Thanks for writing. To be totally honest with you, many modeling schools tell potential clients that they have "the look" because they want your money. If the school wants you to pay $1500.00, will they guarantee her a job when she finishes the class? I suggest that you find a reputable agency with no school attached to the program. If your daughter truly has "the look," they will do the marketing and find work for her. Most agencies without schools will provide your daughter training. It's best to call around and do your homework before making a large investment. The modeling school said that if your daughter joins it, it would improve her self-esteem and improve her grades. If you want your child to have greater self-esteem you might consider looking into self-esteem classes in your area.

Make your fate!

Dr. John Oda
Dear Dr. John:

I'm seventeen years old and having a lot of problems with my mother. She wants me to get out of the house NOW! I'm going to night school to get my GED and I've been earning money as an exotic dancer for the past year. Should I tell my mother my occupation? What should I do?

*Angry in Portland*

Dear Angry:

I want to congratulate you for continuing your education. I think first that you and your mother need to seek some professional help in the mental health field. Also, since you want to gain back trust in your mother, it may not be the best time to tell her about being an exotic dancer. I also feel that a person at seventeen should not live alone. You need to ask yourself several questions.

- Why am I a stripper? What does this occupation give me?
- Am I doing this to build my self-esteem or make quick cash?
- Can this occupation ruin my life? How?
- How will I look and feel in the next five years if I continue this work?
- What can I do to better myself in a positive way and enjoy the benefits?

It best to find an occupation that you can be proud to tell your mother and that makes your feel proud of yourself.

Make your fate!

Dr. John Oda

Dear Dr. John:

I have recently moved to Portland from California. I'm feeling very depressed because of the weather. What should I do?

*Feeling down in Gresham.*

Dear Feeling Down:

The weather should not determine the way you feel. Most people put a label on the way they feel and call it depression. It's only a label. What you say, think and feel you become. It's time to take charge of your life. When you feel depressed move your body in a different way. When you move your body slow and think of all the negative thoughts, you can feel depressed. You can change your focus and stop thinking of the weather and focus on the positive things that are going on in your life. When you change your body movement, it can change your mental, emotional and spiritual state. Depression is only a state, so take control of your life and enjoy your stay. Make today outstanding!

Dr. John Oda

# Services Provided by John Oda

## Oda Research International LLC

A personal development business conducts personal development, sales and corporate seminars that cover a wide range of topics from mastery of communication, personal development, and mental conditioning. www.drjohnoda.com

## Speaking Bureau

Design for youth programs, parenting workshops, schools, colleges, self-esteem, and sales training, corporate events, keynote speakers, leadership for more information please go to  speaker@motivateteens.net

## Bonding the Family Together

This program is a three-day seminar for the entire family that takes you far beyond the old over-used, burned out techniques of the past. Dr. John Oda has dedicated the last seventeen years of his life to discovering the key strategies of the most successful families in the world. At Bonding the Family Together you will be presented with that information in an easy to understand and entertaining manner.

Dr. Oda's Bonding the Family Together Seminar ® is the result of extensive interviewing and the identification of key aspects of modern successful families. The Seminar will equip you to adopt successful bonding strategies through modeling the techniques of families who after moving through tough times, found the ability to bond together. Now you can spend time with Dr. John Oda in person and gain years of this experience in just three days, learning to make these techniques work for your family.

**The Seven Techniques of Highly Self-Motivated Teens**

This two-day program is the foundation for teen success. This program teaches teens the basic steps for accomplishing their goals. This program is a MUST for any teen wanting to achieve success.

**The Seven Principles to Connect with Your Teen**

This two-day program will show parents how to connect with their teen(s). The Seven Principles from the book, this will impact your life forever. http://www.motivateteens.net

# Notes

Printed in the United States
49904LVS00005B/166-237

9 781591 138624